AF863640

ANDRÉS PEREIRA PAZ

RADIO CARABUCO

KÜNSTLERHAUS BETHANIEN KFW STIFTUNG

Preface

Residencies play a key role in today's globalised cultural and intellectual world. They serve as think tanks to reflect and negotiate ideas; they provide work spaces and a setting for creative production and activity. Since 2013, KfW Stiftung has been offering an artist-in-residence programme for emerging visual artists in collaboration with Künstlerhaus Bethanien. The proposals submitted by independent nominators are examined by an expert jury that selects two promising candidates. These artists are then invited to spend one year in Berlin, giving them the opportunity to engage with the city's cultural scene, expand their personal and professional networks and develop their artistic practices. To date, 15 fellows, their exhibitions and the accompanying series of monographs have helped the programme develop into a transnational platform for artistic exploration and transcultural encounter.

This edition of the publication series focuses on Bolivian artist Andrés Pereira Paz and complements his ongoing project *Radio Carabuco*, a collaborative online podcast radio station. The project, developed during the residency, features an immersive installation that was exhibited at Künstlerhaus Bethanien in Berlin before being put on show at Villa 102 by KfW Stiftung in Frankfurt. Pereira Paz uses concepts and images of "hell" to explore processes of demonizing the "other". The artistic investigation of structural consequences of Latin America's colonial heritage is the foundation of the artist's practice. This publication illustrates Pereira Paz's ongoing explorations: it documents and contextualises the current project, provides a broader perspective of Pereira Paz's works and serves as a platform for the artist.

Daniela Leykam and Christoph Tannert
Editors

Contents

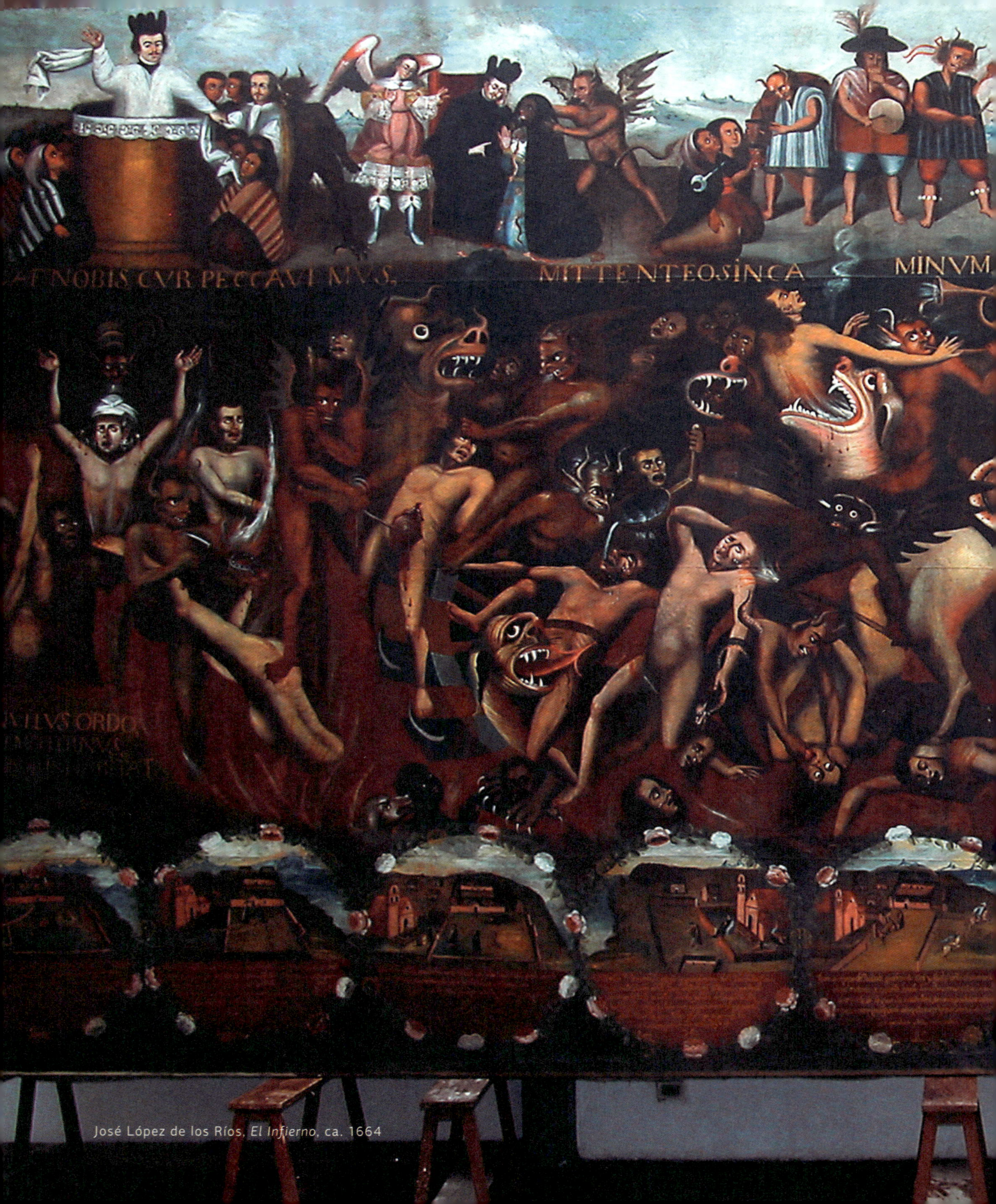

José López de los Ríos, *El Infierno*, ca. 1664

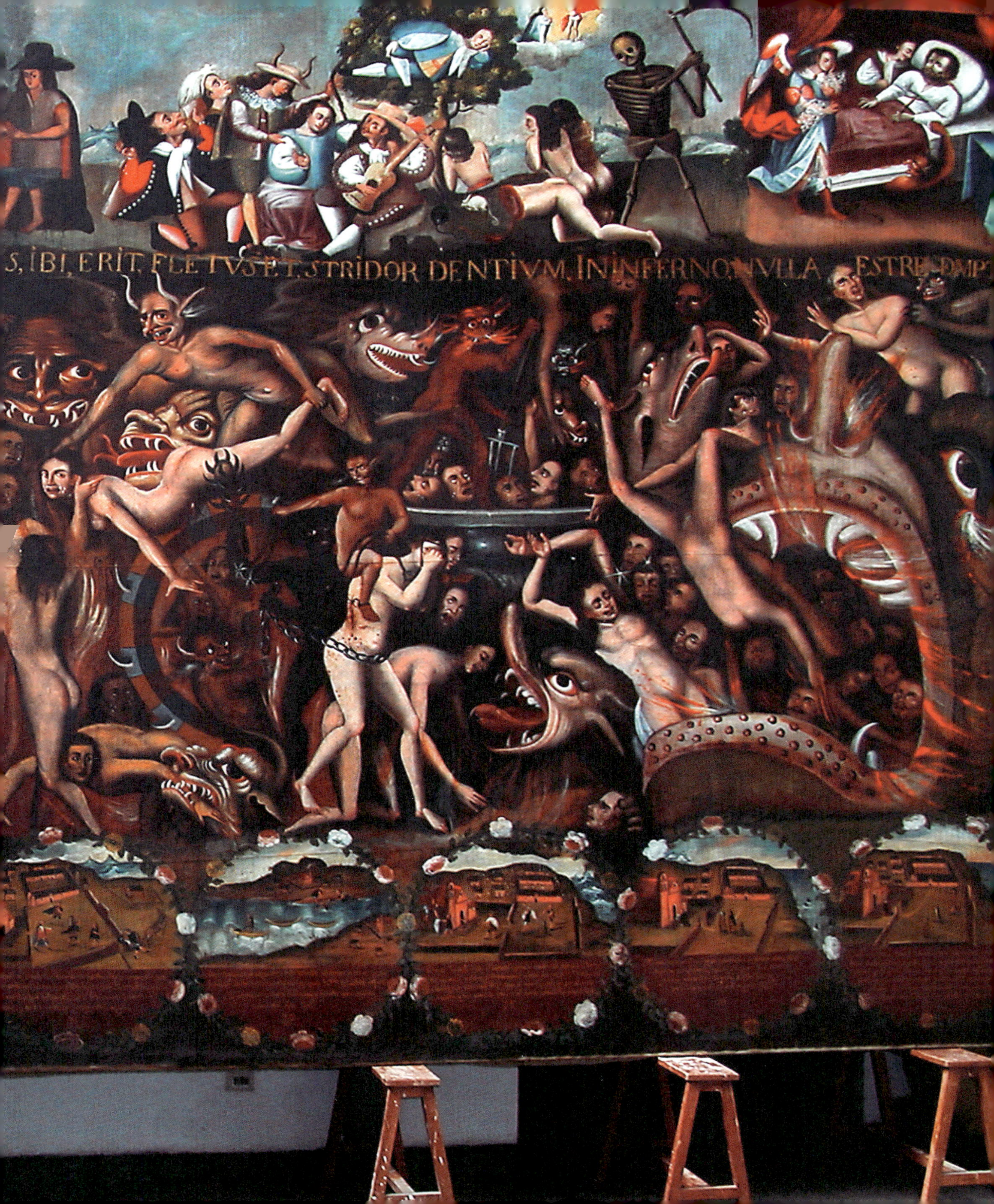
S, IBI, ERIT, FLETVS ET, STRIDOR DENTIVM, IN INFERNO NVLLA ESTRE

Radio Carabuco

Interview by Richard Davey with Andrés Pereira Paz

Around 1664, Joseph de Arellano commissioned José López de Los Ríos to paint the *Four Last Things* for his church in the town of Carabuco on the Bolivian shore of Lake Titicaca. These monumental paintings of *Purgatory, The Last Judgement, Heaven and Hell* were part of the Roman Catholic Church's mission to evangelise the indigenous population of Latin America. Priests like de Arellano travelled deep into inhospitable regions to prove the depth of their faith, whilst also extending the Church's colonial power. The paintings were modelled on a series of 1606 engravings made by the French artist Philippe Thomassin, who, having based himself in Rome, had made a career engraving copies of drawings by Italian artists such as Antonio Tempesta and Giulio Romana. Thomassin's engravings of the *Last Judgement* were particularly popular amongst artists and patrons across the New World, since they gave them easy access to the Christian art of Italy without having to travel or study there.

Although Los Rios's dramatic painting of Hell was not a direct copy of Thomassin's engraving, it did reproduce the essential elements, including the gaping monster's mouth of Hell swallowing up unfortunate sinners, and the writhing mass of winged bestial demons who wrestle with, disembowel and torment unfortunate sinners. Los Rios, however, adapted his European model to the local context. Unconcerned by the Baroque extravaganzas that were then the fashion in Italy and France, his graphic, raw depiction of Hell would have been more familiar to a medieval European audience. The series of vignettes that run above and below the central scene also reflect earlier models, allowing what is universal – the idea of Hell – to be adapted for the particular context of the Church's mission to Bolivia.

The scenes running above the top of the painting explore the consequences of false confession, both in terms of the act of confession and hearing it without true authority to do so. We see an indigenous woman standing before a Jesuit priest confessing her sins, yet her black face and the presence of a devil and coiled snake beside her suggest that this is a false confession. Further along the painting a *hechicero*, one of the indigenous shamans, hears the confession of two women, whilst other *hechiceros*, signified by drums, encourage the people to dance. Such native confessions and dancing were considered highly undesirable and sinful by the Jesuit missionaries. The purpose of the painting was to show those contemplating it what would happen if they didn't repent – the inevitable descent into Hell.

Along the bottom, a series of roundels recount the story of how the Apostle St Bartholomew appeared in the region of Lake Titicaca at the time of Christ, and, having defeated a demon and shaman, converted the first indigenous apostle of the Andes, who erected a miraculous cross in Carabuco.

While the graphic horrors of Hell were certainly enough to terrify and intimidate the indigenous population, the roundels add to the colonial power play by telling the story of the Apostle to the Andes and the origins of the Carabuco Cross in words as well as images. Just as the small number of Incan nobility had once exerted their power over the masses through written language, now the Church did the same, forcing the largely illiterate population to access the full mysteries of faith through the clergy, who were the only ones who could read, write and speak Latin or Spanish.

A reproduction of Los Rios's painting provides the focus for Andrés Pereira Paz's exhibition *Radio Carabuco* at Künstlerhaus Bethanien, Berlin, where it is projected onto rich scarlet walls. Hanging alongside it is a series of photographs that chronicle the *Chinas Morenas* transvestites, who for many years participated in the carnival celebrations in Bolivia until the government prohibited their participation. Suspended from the ceiling are a number of brass line sculptures that use the profiles of the demons that can be seen in both the painting and the print as their starting point. Headphones then allow visitors to listen to the series of podcasts that Pereira Paz has recorded with friends to explore themes that respond to the Carabuco painting.

Richard Davey: When did you first become aware of the Carabuco painting of Hell?

Andrés Pereira Paz: I've known it since my childhood. There are two really well-known representations of Hell in Bolivian art, and this is one of them. Not everyone knows it, but if you come from a middle-class Catholic family, as I do, then you will inevitably be aware of it. I saw it quite a lot as a child because my parents would often take us up into the mountains during Holy Week to visit churches and watch the Fiesta celebrations.

RD: It's such a striking image, which reminds me of medieval European sculptures and paintings. Like them, its realism is not about anatomical correctness and perfection but about conveying its message through an immediate and emotional intensity. It's definitely intended to put the fear of God – or rather, the fear of Hell – into those looking at it.

APP: What I find interesting is where the artist situates Hell. In the original print it sits at the bottom of the composition, beneath the Last Judgement and Heaven, but in the painting it occupies a large place in the middle, between the story of how the first Apostle of the Andes was converted and more contemporary scenes at the top where you see Jesuit priests preaching and hearing confessions and indigenous shamans encouraging the people to dance and listening to confessions as well.

RD: So although Hell is shown as being "down there" – underground, as you'd expect –, it is unusually placed in the middle, not at the bottom, in the space between, where earth is normally situated.

APP: Yes. But what makes it interesting for me is that it is seen as being under the earth. Mining was the main industry in Bolivia and especially in the mountainous areas around Carabuco, and so the relationship with the earth was totally different. *Pachamama* (Mother Earth) was seen as something fertile and good, producing silver and precious metals as well as being a major provider of food and other riches. You needed to treat it well: with respect. If you did so, it would reward you. But when the Spaniards came, they told the people to extract as much of the precious resources as possible, to exhaust what was there. They also told them that *Pachamama* was evil; it was Hell. So there was a clash of cultures.

RD: And this is what you see in the painting. The gaping "Hell mouth" is not just an entry into the Underworld, for those used to a life of mining it would have looked like a mine entrance. What was once seen as a way to access good things has now become monstrous, leading to terror and death.

APP: Guamán Poma de Ayala, an indigenous chronicler writing about the conquest, said that with the coming of the Spanish, "the world had turned upside down" and this painting shows it. What the indigenous people had once held sacred was demonised. What was good had become evil.

RD: So your new work, *Radio Carabuco*, is about the imposition of colonial power and its effects?

APP: To an extent, yes. It's about control and imposing one set of values over another – if you don't believe in our God, this is what happens. But I'm not trying to criticise the Catholic Church. I grew up in a Catholic country and went to a Jesuit school. I deliberately entered into dialogue with this painting because it is part of my country's art history, and I also chose it because it's about Hell.

RD: That's an interesting starting point in this very secular world. When fewer people say that they believe in God, why would you want to focus on the idea of Hell?

APP: Firstly, I would say that we are all spiritual beings,

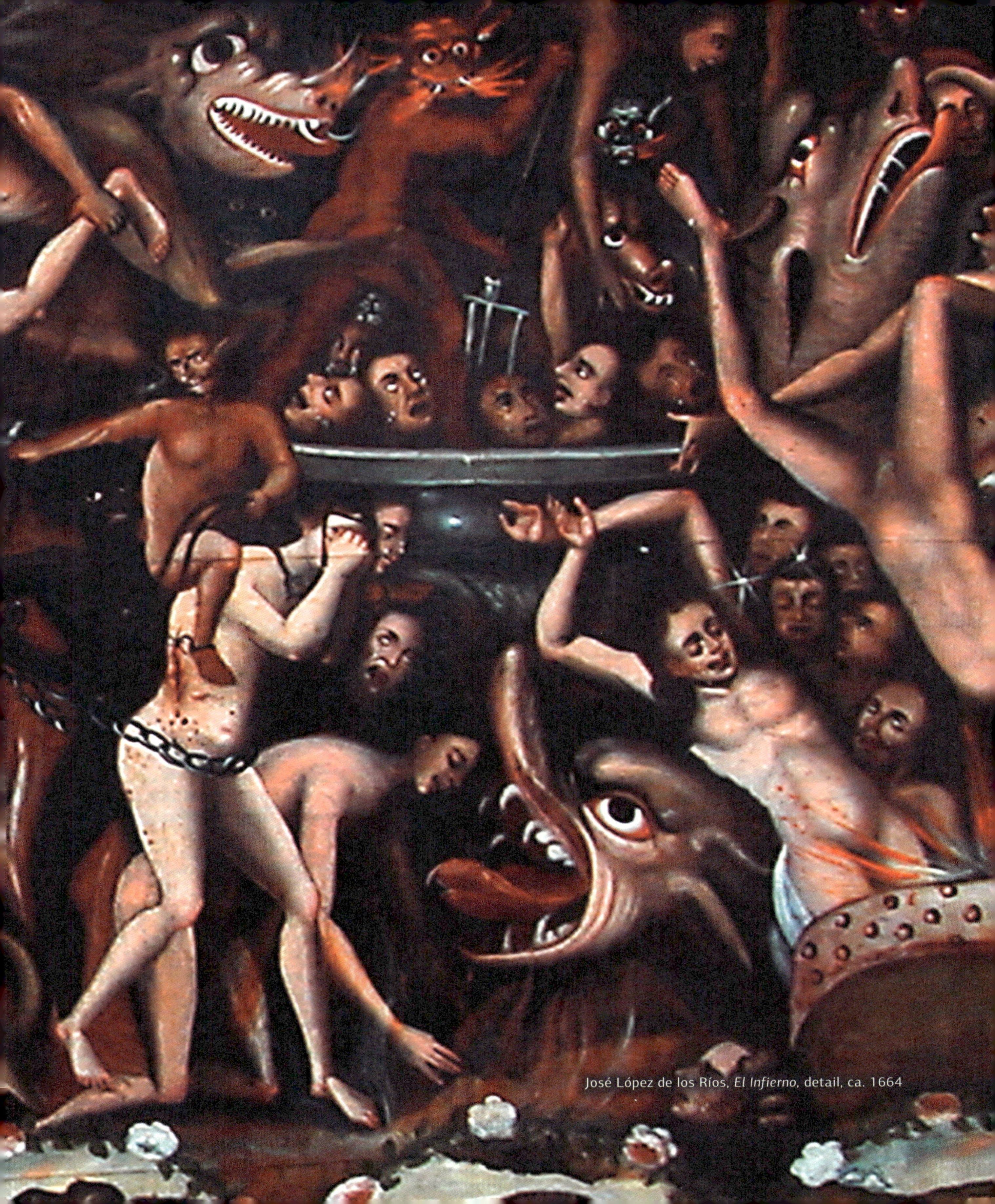

José López de los Ríos, *El Infierno*, detail, ca. 1664

and therefore it should still have relevance. But I also think the idea of Hell has a particular resonance right now. Hell is full of demons, and our world is defined by demonisation, almost more than ever before. The way people are represented in the media or social media is so often negative. People are demonising each other, and they're particularly attacking the "other". Even in Berlin, which is very progressive in many ways, everything is polarised. We're on a quest for black or white, right or wrong. Just look at what's happening with Islamophobia, and the way media has demonised Muslims. And look at America. President Trump is constantly playing on people's fears about the "other": demonising Mexican immigrants, Iran, North Korea. For me, there is nothing more emblematic of what's happening today than this 350-year-old painting.

RD: But what's interesting about this painting is that it places Hell in the middle, not on the edge. Instead of the usual opposition between Heaven and Hell, one extreme or the other, it sits between scenes of everyday life. That central space, neither one thing nor the other, seems to me to be really important in this painting and in your work. It's a role that artists often play: occupying the gaps in society; looking, without taking extreme positions. It also seems to me that the podcasts that have been created for *Radio Carabuco* are also concerned with those who may seem to exist on the margins, but actually occupy an in-between space. And to an extent, that is the space you occupy, living as an artist in Berlin, but coming from Bolivia.

APP: And in Bolivia I occupy that same in-between space. Because sixty-five percent of the population are indigenous, and I'm a mixed-race person. To an extent, my family are also part of the immigrant colonisers and European refugees who came to this country. There's a word in the Aymara language – *chi'xi* – which means neither one thing nor the other, and I'm really interested in this idea. I had a teacher in Buenos Aires who taught us that art is like living on the border of a drawing. Just as the media are the space between people and politics, so artists need to occupy the space between people and the metaphysical.

RD: I think this can be seen in your approach to this exhibition. Rather than it being all about you, you've collaborated with a number of people to create these podcasts. Therefore it's not about the "I" of the artist, working on his own to make a unique work of art, but about the "we" of collaboration, where your role is the act of creation that exists in the space between the different collaborators, bringing and holding them together.

APP: Berlin is such a progressive city, with lots of collectives, groups and collaboration, and I thought the best way to address this was to work collectively. Like many people living in South America, I grew up with a colonial mindset. We always think we're behind everyone else, so I began to work in dialogue with other artists that I knew so that I wasn't always looking elsewhere to validate what I was doing. This time, the collaboration was with different social scientists, activists and friends from different parts of the world. There was an Argentinian painter who said that they don't do research that takes them more than one square metre away from where they are. I like that idea. I collaborated with people whose voices, talents and points of view I found interesting for the project. I just gave them the rules of the game and allowed them to get on with it.

RD: The podcasts that have been produced are fascinating insights into your dialogue with the different perspectives of your various collaborators, and I think we see this commitment to the interweaving of viewpoints in the subjects themselves, where either you're looking at those people or things that occupy the intersections of life, bridging the gap between people or genders, or you're creating fictions that are also factual. But whilst the audios are collaborative, we specifically see your input in the final exhibition. Your use of red walls is incredibly striking, staining everything, including the projected reproduction of the painting, with a hellish aura as if they had been soaked in blood or set on fire.

APP: Yes, but there's another reason I used red as well. One of the things I've learnt living in Berlin is that Germans find red places cosy, and I like the idea of turning things on their head just as the painting does: so that a place that looks at the idea of Hell, demons and hate subconsciously feels safe and comfortable.

RD: And then hanging suspended from the ceiling are these sculptures based on the profiles of demons which we can see in the painting and the print, and they not only gleam, but they occupy the middle ground of the space, just like Hell occupies the middle ground in the painting.

APP: They have a real sense of presence for me. They're made from brass – I couldn't afford gold –, as I wanted something that suggested mining and therefore related to the painting and its association of Hell with mining and the earth. And it's not just these demon sculptures; there are also whips hanging from the ceiling. In indigenous communities in Bolivia, the leaders are given whips to represent their authority, so they suggest both pain and control ...

RD: ... which is what the painting of Hell was about: control through the threat of pain.

APP: Yes. Exactly. I've also included some small golden skulls in the space, with cigarettes for mouths and beer bottle tops for eyes, and I've called them the "Berliners". I wanted to change the gravity of the space, and these suspended pieces do this. They move a lot as people walk through, and then as people stay in the room and listen to the podcasts, it doesn't feel like the usual exhibition space.

RD: I agree. The suspended, moving pieces make us interact with the space differently. We encounter it as physical space rather than as a passive space, which we go into to look at things. The red enhances this, it has a visceral quality, and then you make us listen to things, and what I find really interesting is that you reintroduce the importance of the oral tradition which the Jesuit missionaries had tried to take away through the imposition of the written word as the vehicle for transmitting truth.

APP: Radios are really important in Bolivia. More than the internet. Everyone has a radio and listens to it. It's the dominant form of media, bridging the space between peoples and communicating across vast distances, reaching even "the profound" – just like Hell.

RD: I also see this visceral, physical quality in the painting, which is much more about creating a sense of space through what "looks" right, rather than through precise perspectival geometry, as European painters were doing. And the bodily aspect of the painting that you allow us to draw out through your multi-sensory exhibition is a reminder that the painting was always a part of a multi-sensory liturgy, experienced through movement, singing, incense and the taste of the bread and wine in communion.

APP: Absolutely.

RD: And that's what is so refreshing in your work *Radio Carabuco*. That in this conversation between two seemingly different approaches to making art, you allow us to see both in a new light. You not only show us the painterliness of the installation and the physical, multi-sensory nature of the painting, but also that a Baroque Bolivian religious painting can have a universal, contemporary relevance, no longer the exclusive subject of art history but something that speaks to everyday experience.

APP: Exactly, therefore the radio is online at www.radiocarabuco.com and is also designed to reach as many unknown visitors as possible! And hopefully it's just the beginning. Thanks a lot Richard.

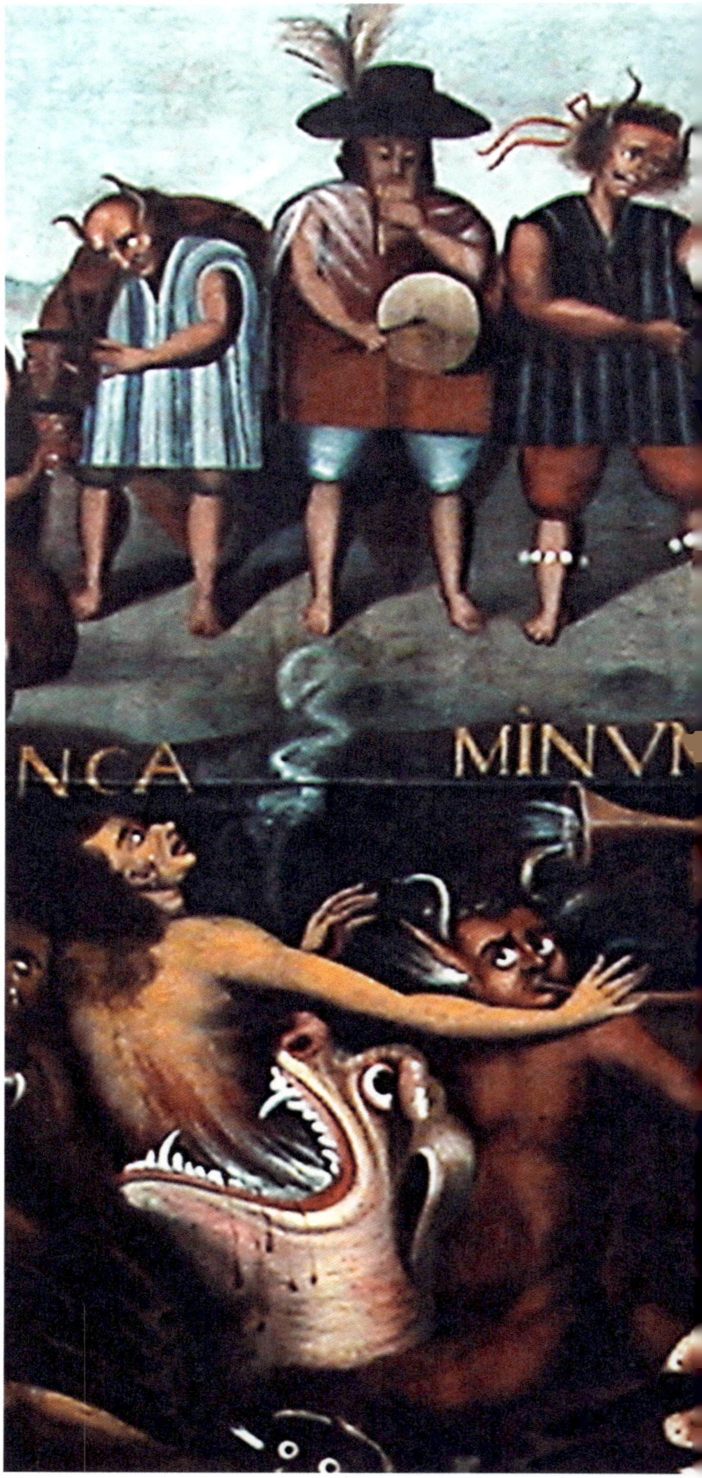

José López de los Ríos, *El Infierno*, detail, ca. 1664

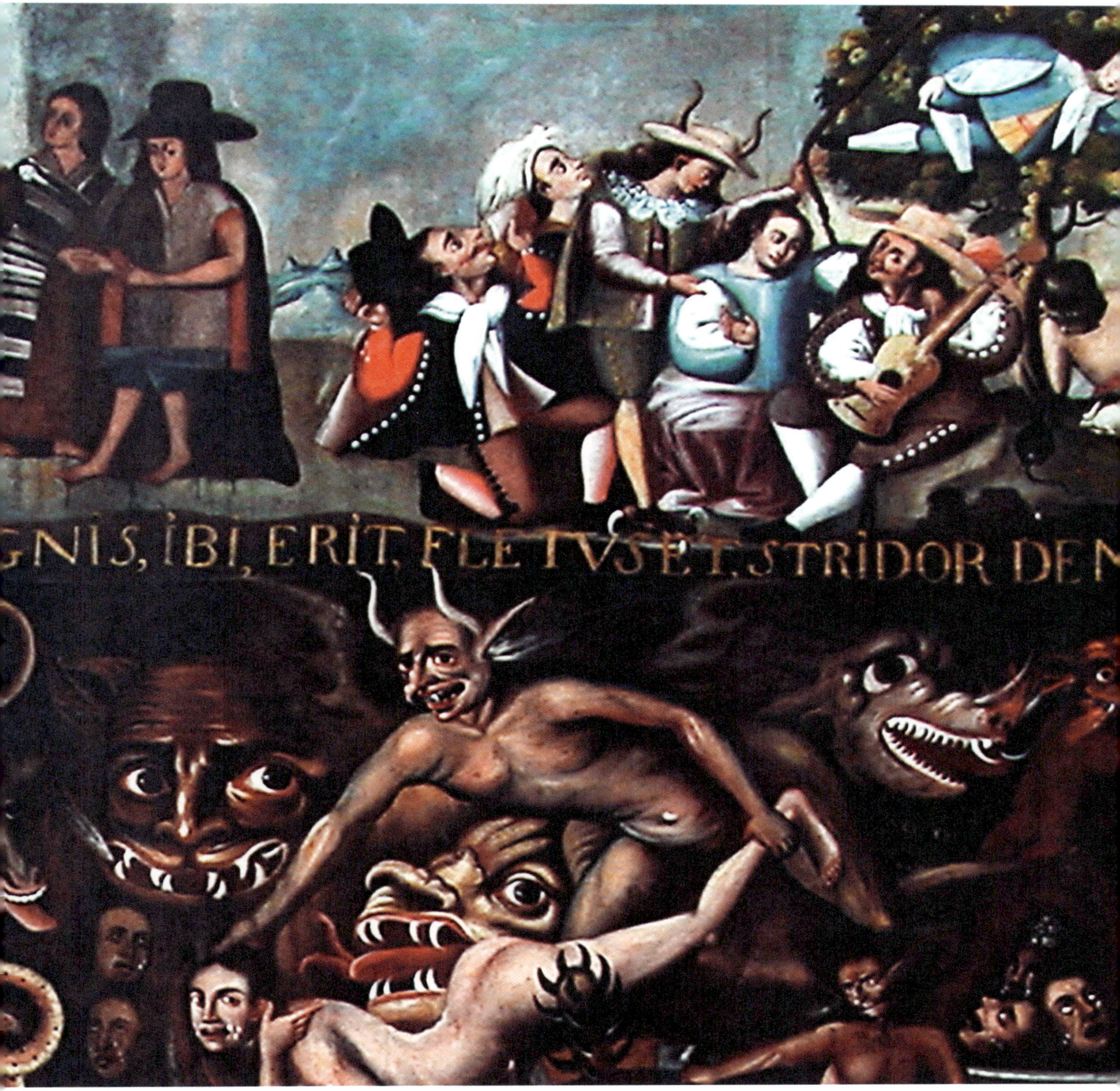
GNIS, IBI, ERIT, FLETVS ET, STRIDOR DEN

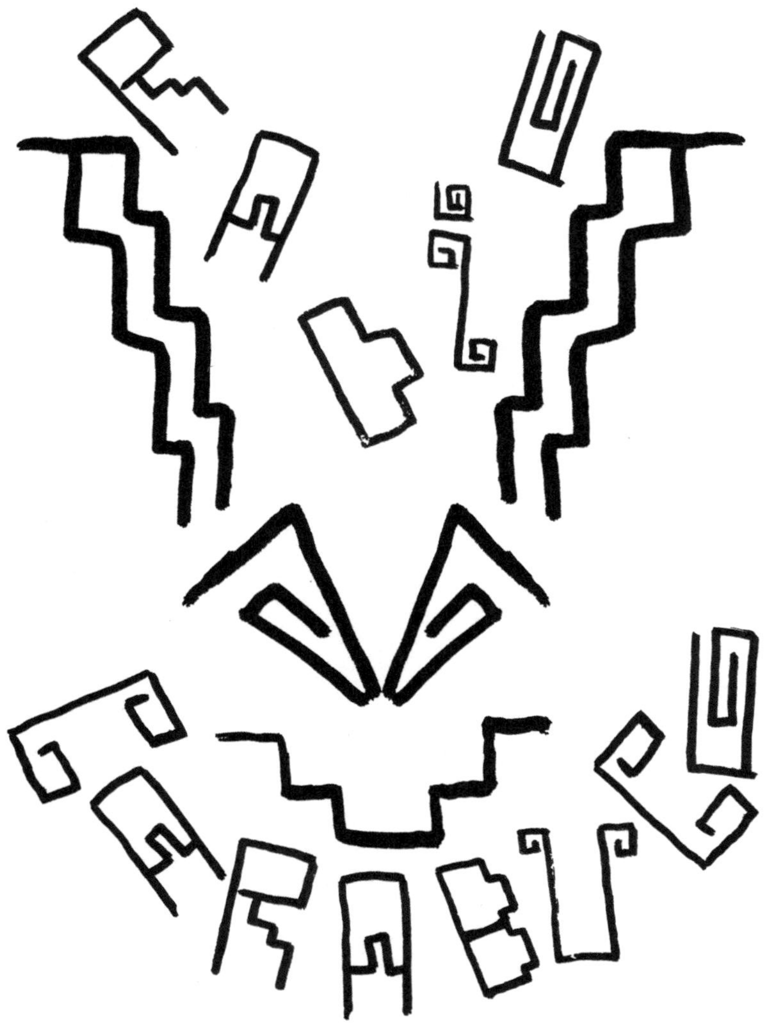

All of the audio pieces and podcasts can be found online at:

www.radiocarabuco.com

Audio pieces in the exhibition by segments
on the following pages

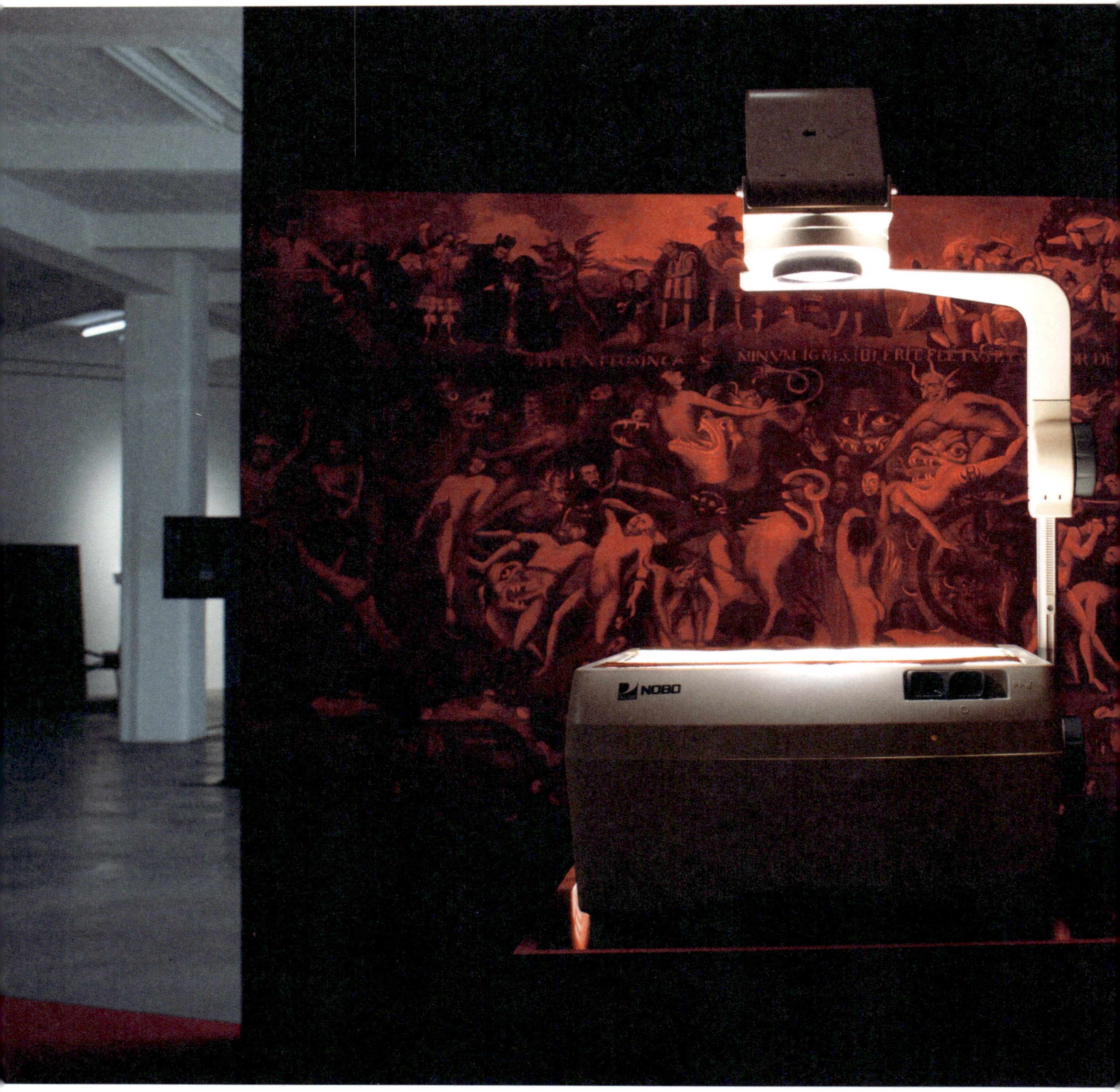
NOBO

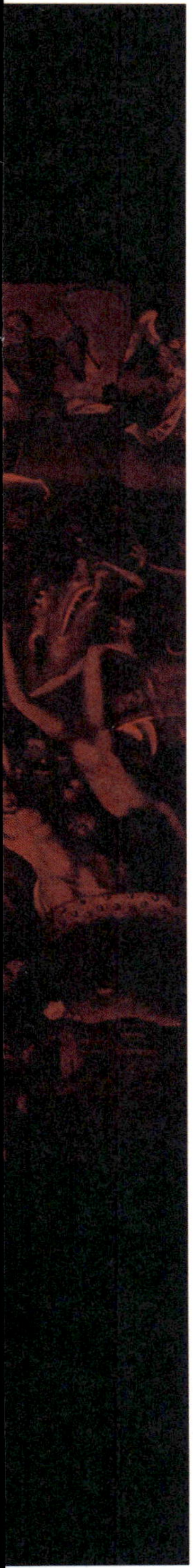

1. Dancing with the Devil

Chinas Morenas in Bolivian folklore, based on an interview with David Aruquipa Pérez broadcast by Andrés Pereira Paz

Audio / 01:04:00

Synopsis: In Bolivia, popular festivities can be seen throughout the country every day of the year. One of the main dances in Bolivian folklore is the *Morenada*. The origins of the *Morenada* can be traced back to the African-American slaves that were imported to work in mining mostly in Potosí, Bolivia. During the early 1960s, folklorist dancer Carlos Espinoza added a new cross-dressing character called Ofelia to the *Morenada* traditional dance. Following the creation of Ofelia, a movement began that changed the folkloric performances and outfits by queering traditional dancing moves and costumes. As these costumes and aesthetics developed, skirts became shorter and boots got higher, so that a glamorous group of *Chinas Morenas* danced at the Oruro Carnival and at the El Señor del Gran Poder festival in La Paz as early as the 1970s. This movement of fabulous *Chinas Morenas* included Barbarella (Peter Alaiza), Titina, Diego Marangani, Candy, Juana, Rommy and Lucha, who are pictured in the photographs in the exhibition space. After being banned by the dictator Hugo Bánzer Suarez in 1985, it was not before the early 2000s that the cross-dressing collective *La Familia Galán* managed to bring back these intriguing characters into the streets of La Paz, this time performing the *Kullawada* dance.

David Aruquipa Pérez is an activist, author, performer and researcher who lives and works in La Paz, Bolivia.

Radio Carabuco, installation view, 2019

2. Right, Right, Right

Right-wing Frankenstein, by Liv Schulman

Audio / 00:26:08

Synopsis: While the world faces a crisis in terms of the extinction of different species, right-wing leaders all over the world are on the rise with a mission of demonising the “other” at a moment in history at which boundaries become blurred. Against this background, *Radio Carabuco* invited the French-Argentinian artist Liv Schulman to stage a parody of right-wing leaders from different parts of Europe fused into one person. In this episode, Schulman plays Frauke Petry (Die blaue Partei, formerly AfD, Germany), Matteo Salvini (Lega Nord, Italy) and Marine Le Pen (Rassemblement National, France). To this end, *Radio Carabuco* borrowed questions from different interviews found on YouTube (Tim Sebastian for Conflict Zone at DW, Andrew Marr for BBC News and Stephen Sackur for HARDtalk).

Liv Schulman is an artist who lives and works in Paris, France and Buenos Aires, Argentina.

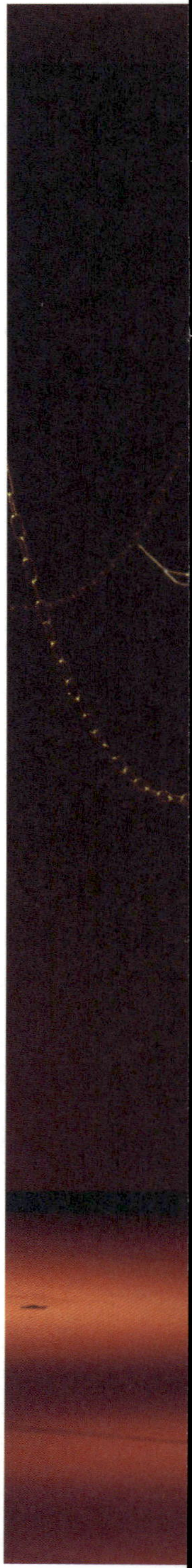

Radio Carabuco, installation view, 2019

Pages 22–35: *Radio Carabuco*, details, 2019

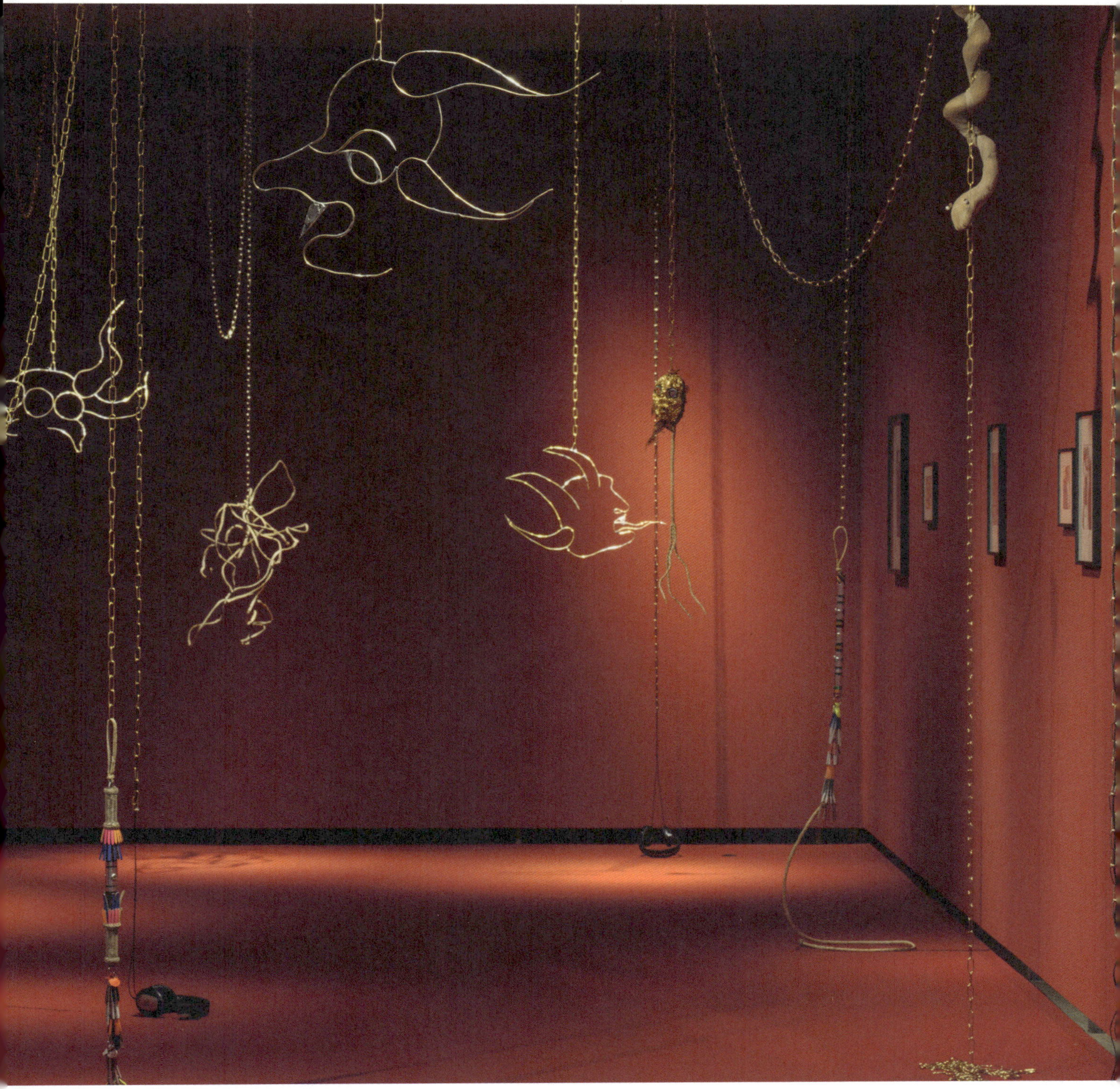

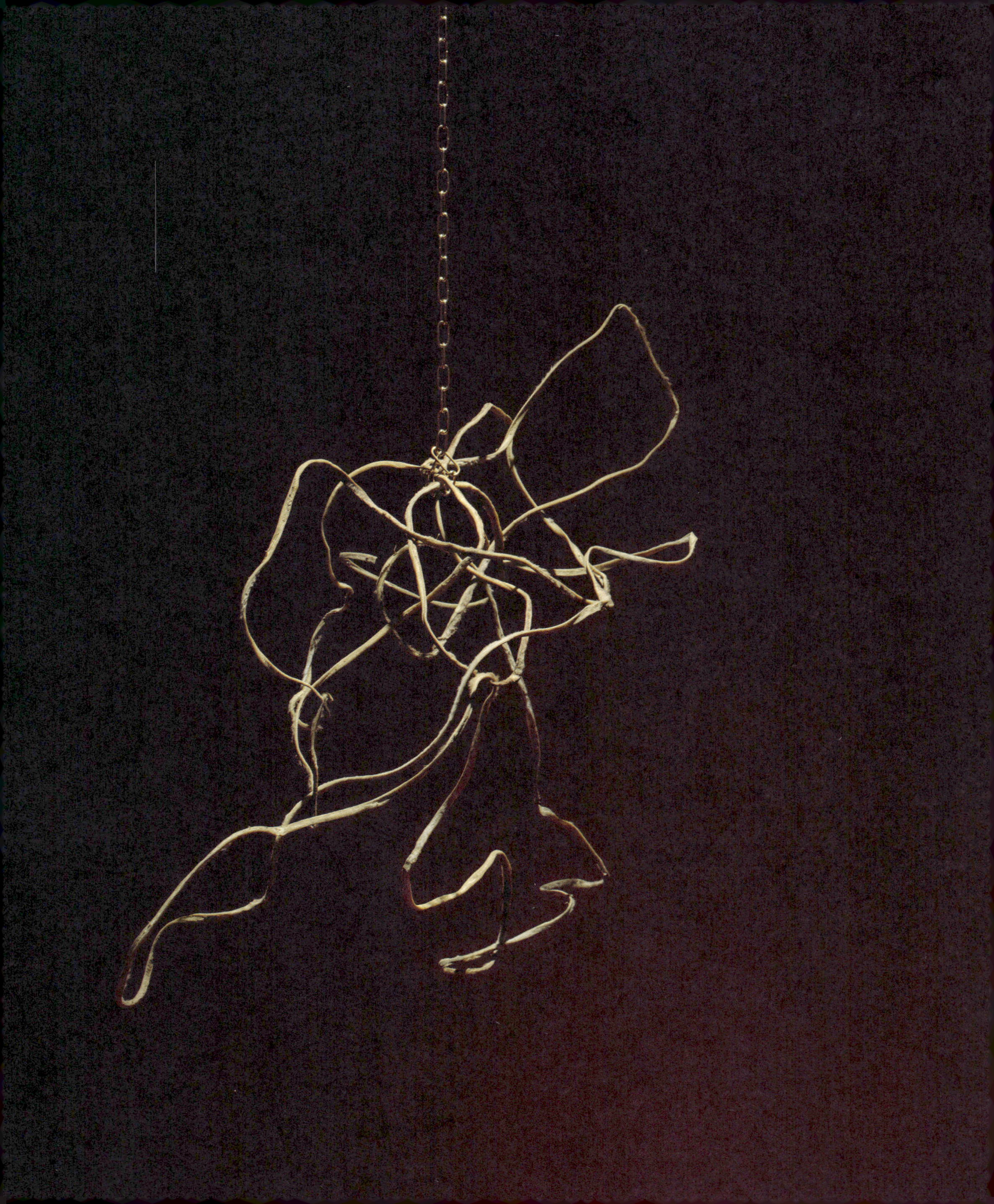

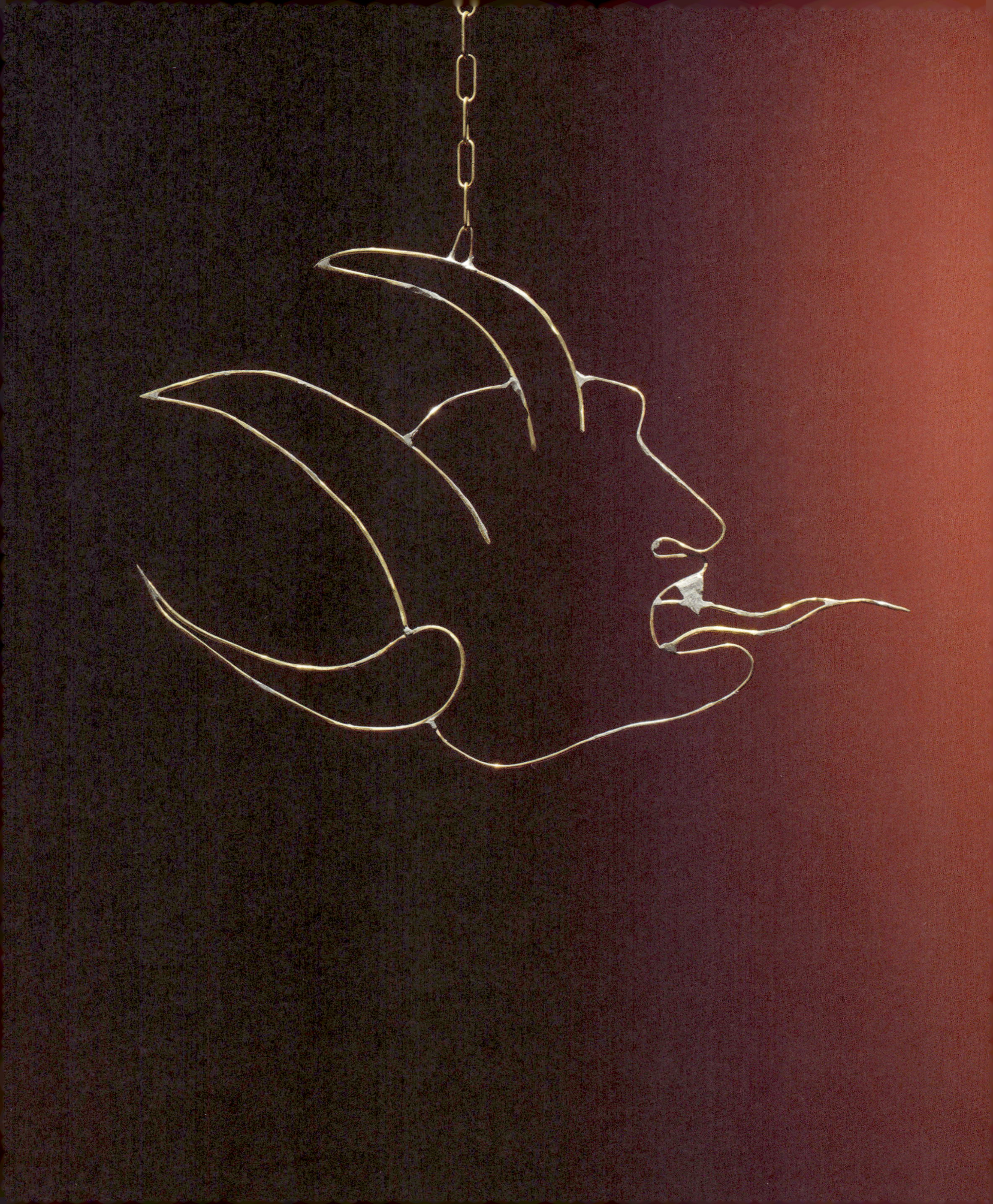

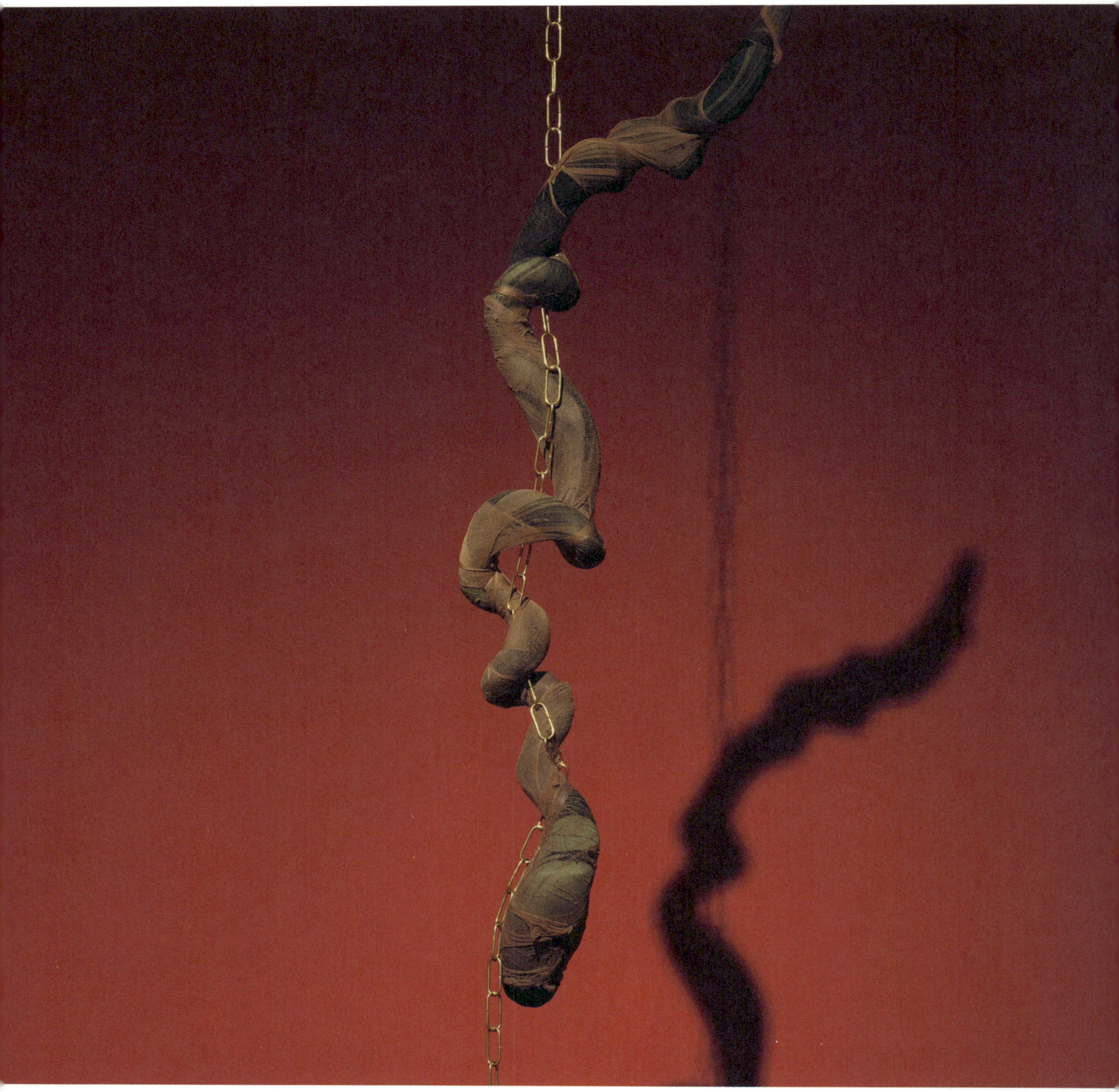

3. My Journey to Hell

Rosa Jane Damiana Fonda, by Gabriel Acevedo Velarde

Audio / 00:05:08

Synopsis: During the 1990s, a star was born in the Bolivian evangelical scene. Priestess Rosa Damiana started a trend of testimonies on the early Bolivian evangelical radio stations. In her original testimony, Rosa Damiana describes her journeys to heaven and hell.

Radio Carabuco commissioned the artist Gabriel Acevedo Velarde to create an audio piece. The artist mixed Rosa Damiana's testimony with Jane Fonda's workout music, leaving listeners with the impression that bodies in hell would be doing constant exercise and have a deeply erotic relationship with "the forbidden".

Gabriel Acevedo Velarde is an artist who lives and works in Lima, Peru.

4. María Mercedes II

María Mercedes arrives in Berlin, performed by Elia Nurvista and Andrés Pereira Paz

Audio / 00:18:27

Synopsis: *María Mercedes* is a Mexican telenovela produced by Valentín Pimstein for Televisa in 1992. It was based on the story *Enamorada* by Inés Rodena. The original telenovela deals with the struggles of a young girl who works in a rich man's house until, after many twists and turns, they fall in love with each other. For *Radio Carabuco*, a second, apocryphal version of the saga is brought to life as a "radionovela" performed by Indonesian artist Elia Nurvista (María Mercedes II) and Bolivian artist Andrés Pereira Paz (Pulgoso the Dog). This time, María Mercedes is a struggling young artist who wants to make it in Berlin's dynamic art scene.

Elia Nurvista is an artist and activist who lives and works in Berlin, Germany, and Yogyakarta, Indonesia.

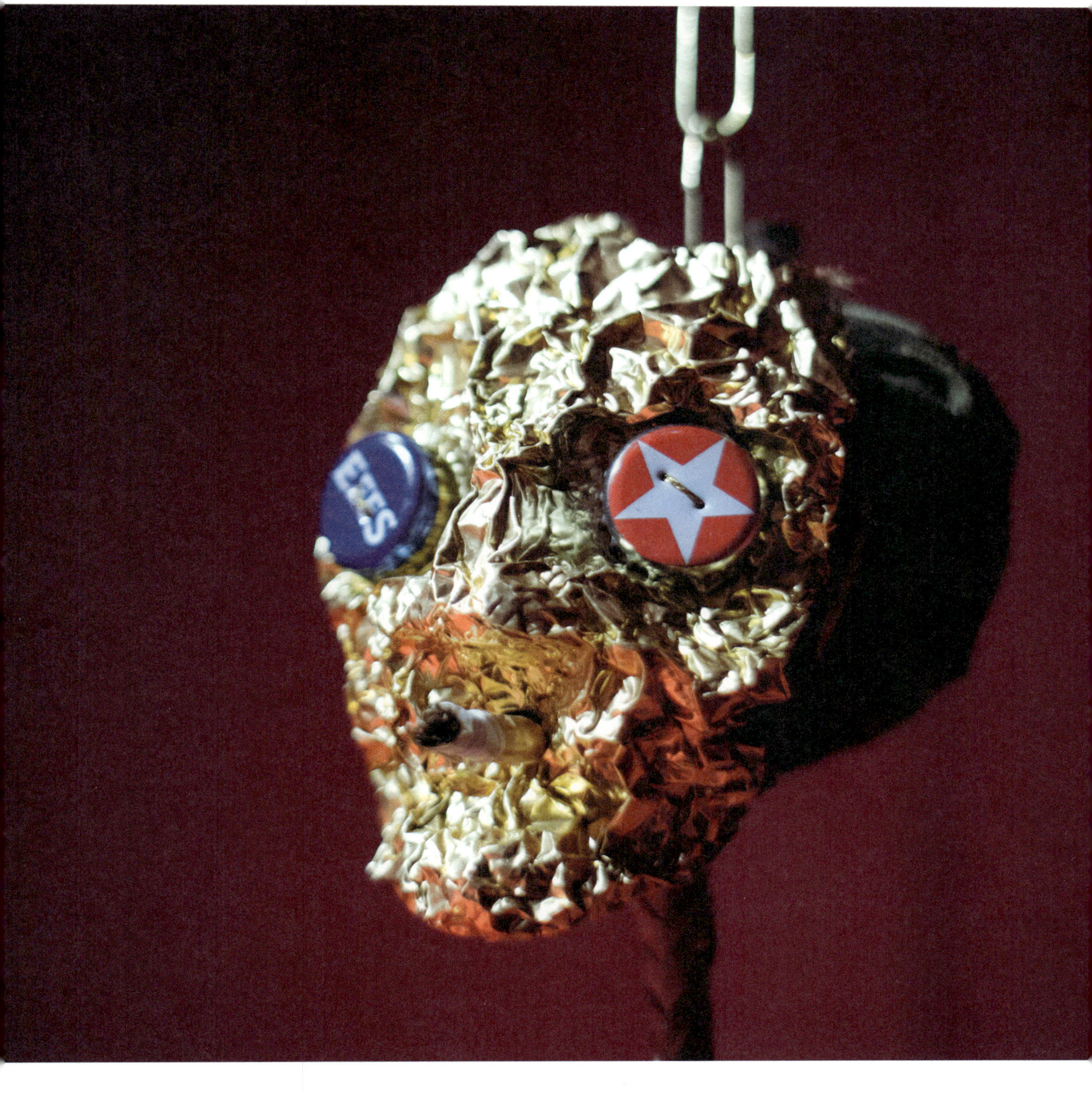

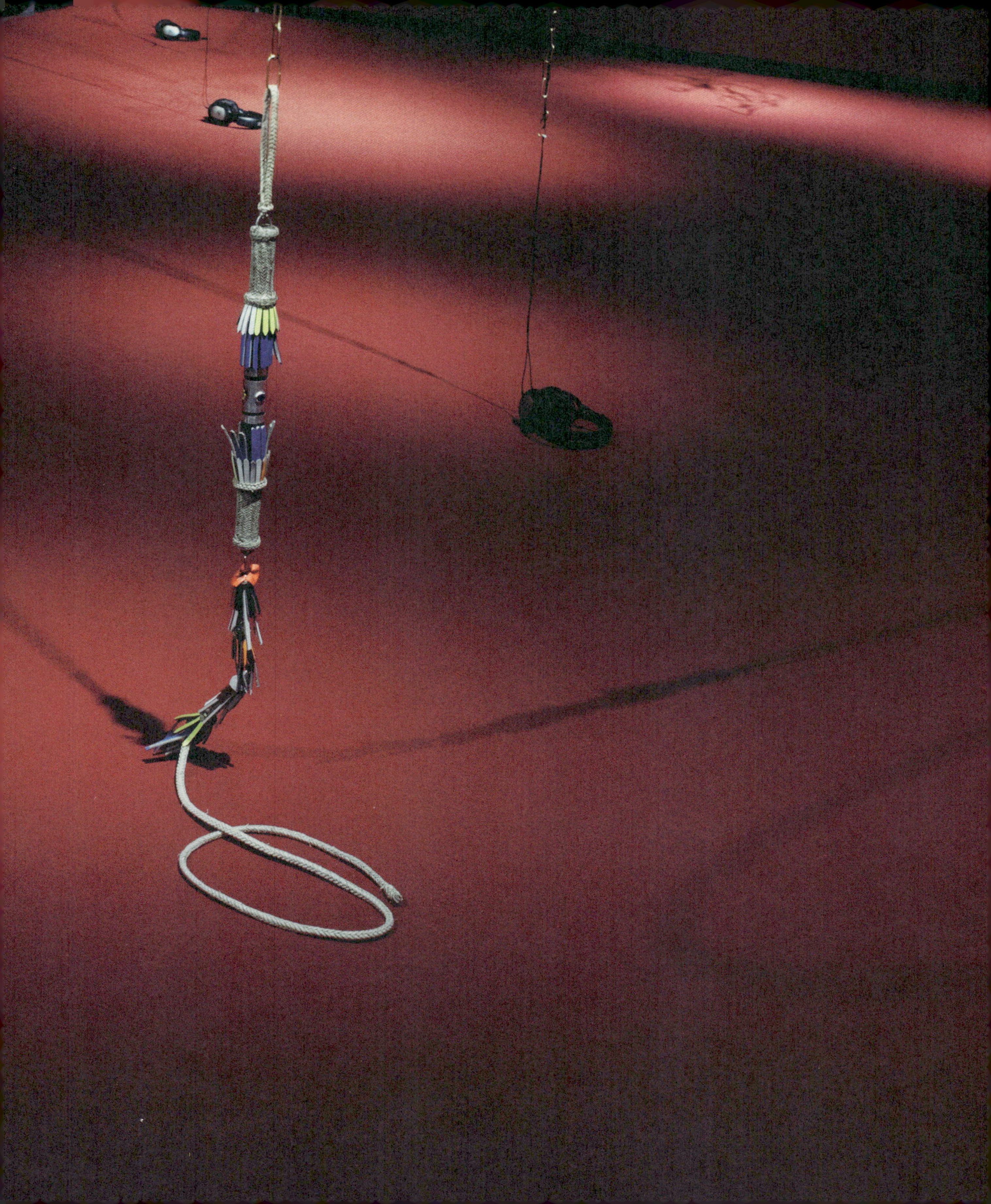

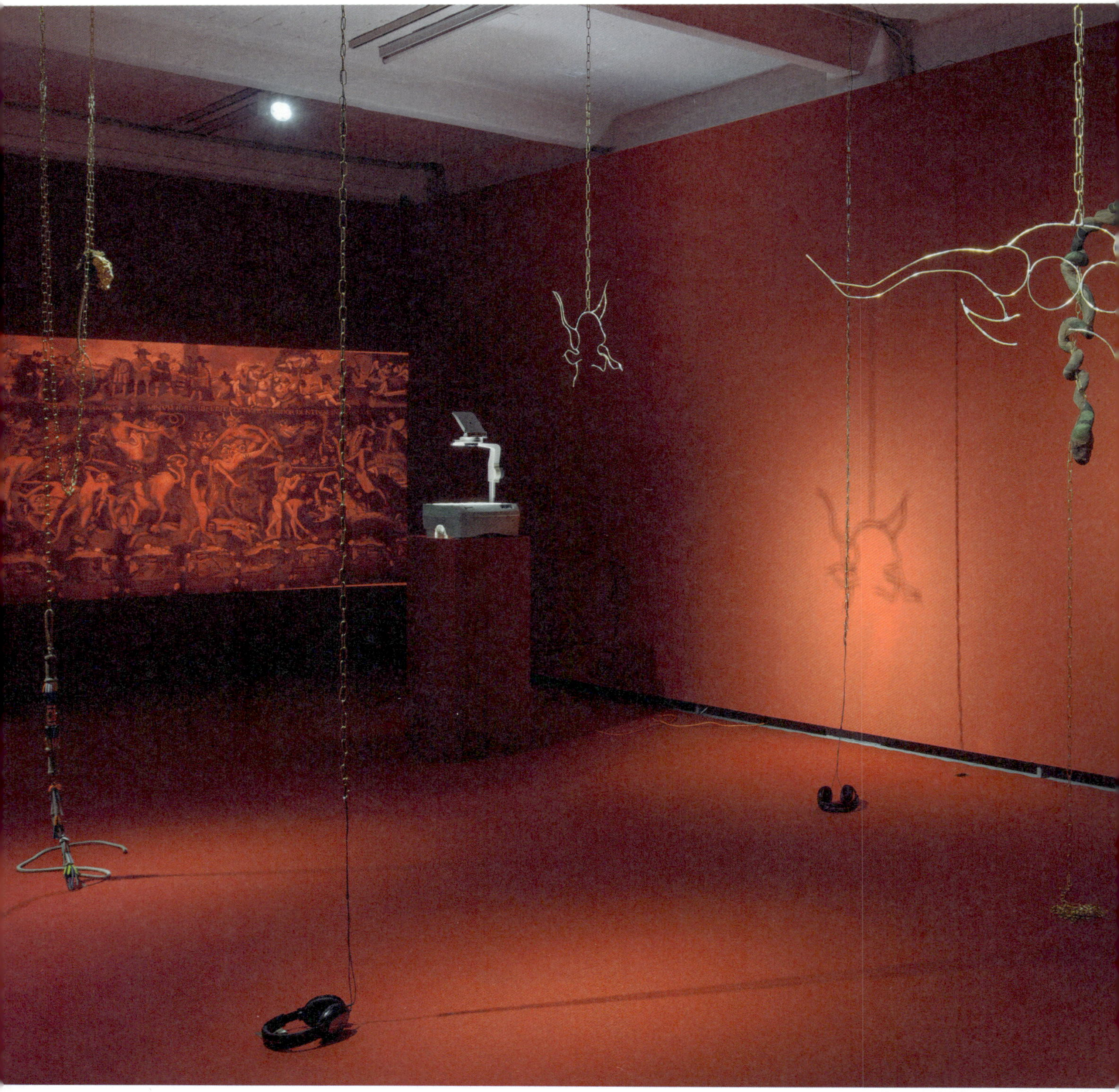

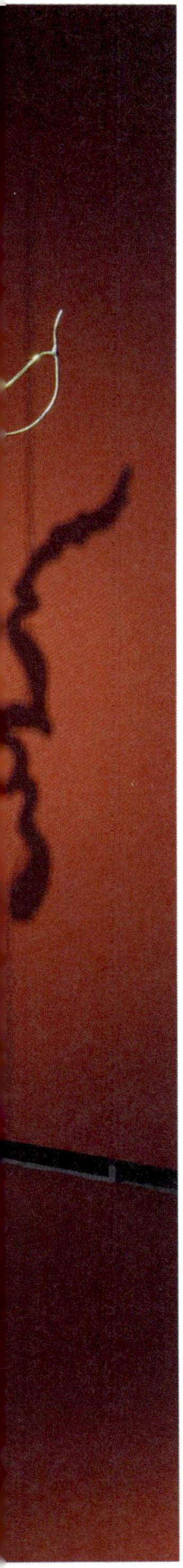

5. Extractivisms

Blood of the Earth, by Ana Alenso

Audio / 00:09:31

Synopsis: This audio piece by artist Ana Alenso mixes a range of sounds related to oil and the extractive exploitation of natural resources in Latin America, an activity which started with the colonial period and has continued ever since. Alenso combines original sounds from an industrial context with samples of Venezuelan music such as the traditional Fulia Barloventeña song "Oye la mar como suena" (Hey, How Does the Ocean Sound) and "Of the Word God" by The Books 2. The piece also includes excerpts from a talk given by Terry Lynn Karl on the topic of "Democracy, Governance and War in Oil Exporting Nations" at the University of Chicago, which addresses the ideas held by Colombia's indigenous U'wa tribe, who regard oil as Earth's blood, as well as quotes of the Venezuelan politician Juan Pablo Pérez Alfonso, who referred to oil as "the excrement of the devil".

This interplay of different elements paints a vivid picture of the effects and points of view surrounding natural resources in a local context, which can sometimes appear contradictory or at odds with each other. However, the piece exposes the exploitation of resources by the West and the potential consequences of these activities for Latin America.

Ana Alenso is a Venezuelan artist based in Berlin, Germany.

6. Radio Stories

Popular Bolivian radio and social conflicts
A conversation between Stanislaw Czaplicky and Andrés Pereira Paz

Audio / 00:56:50

Synopsis: The role played by media is continuously changing and evolving. Western democracies and historically oppressed minority populations have come under pressure by the medias' control over social subjectivity during specific events (such as elections). In Bolivia, the radio has played a key role in social conflicts and has proven to be an effective means of mass coordination and articulation as well as an interactive medium that facilitates communication between groups. In this podcast, Stanislaw Czaplicky examines the impact radio had at three key moments in Bolivia's contemporary struggle against both the national and the transnational management of natural resources: the Water War (2000), the Gas War (2003) and the recent TIPNIS conflict between indigenous communities and the government in the Bolivian Amazon.

Stanislaw Czaplicky is a Bolivian-Polish economist, activist and street artist, who lives and works in Berlin, Germany.

Radio Carabuco, installation view, images from the David Aruquipa-Comunidad Diversidad photographic archive, 2019

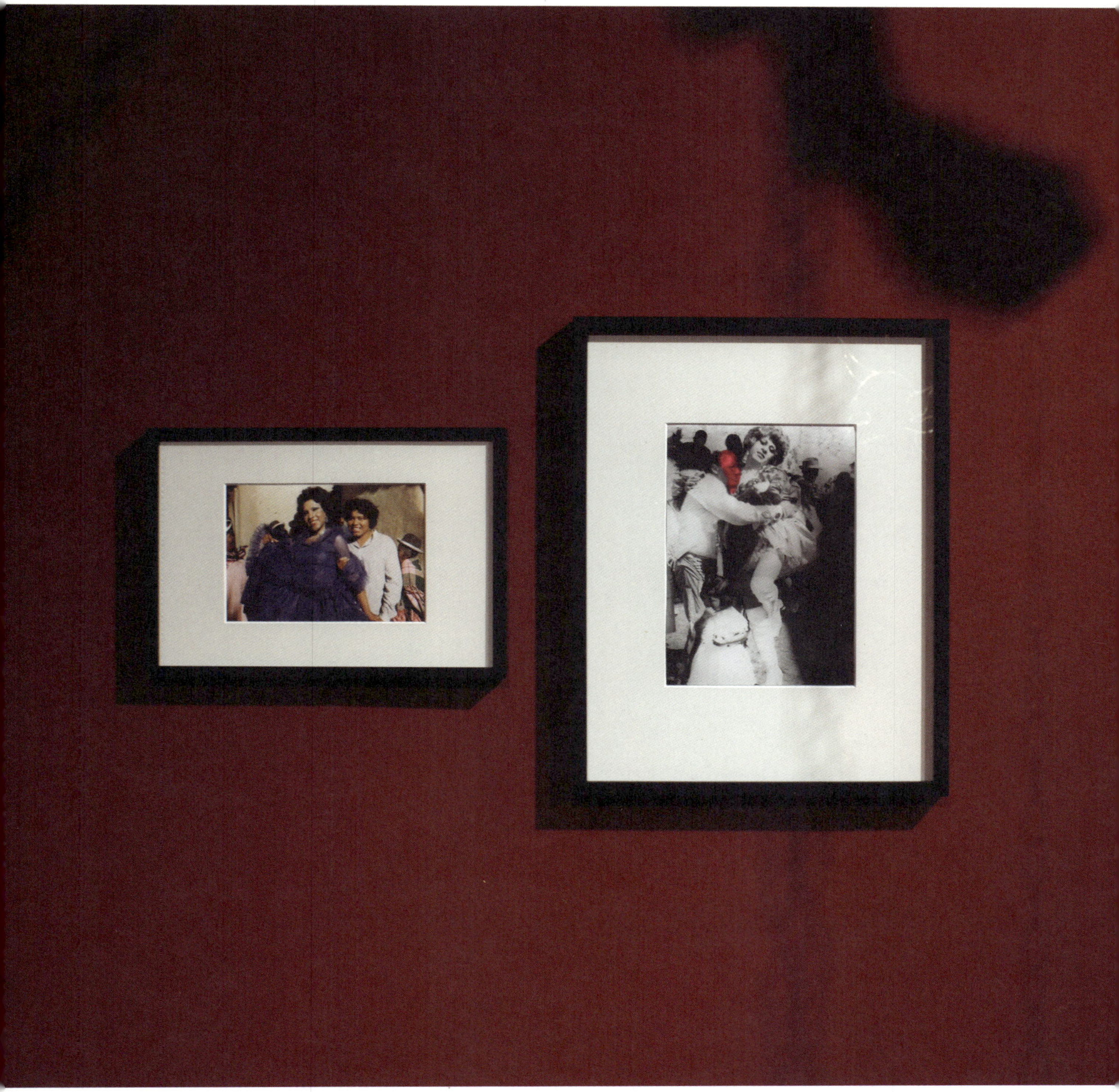

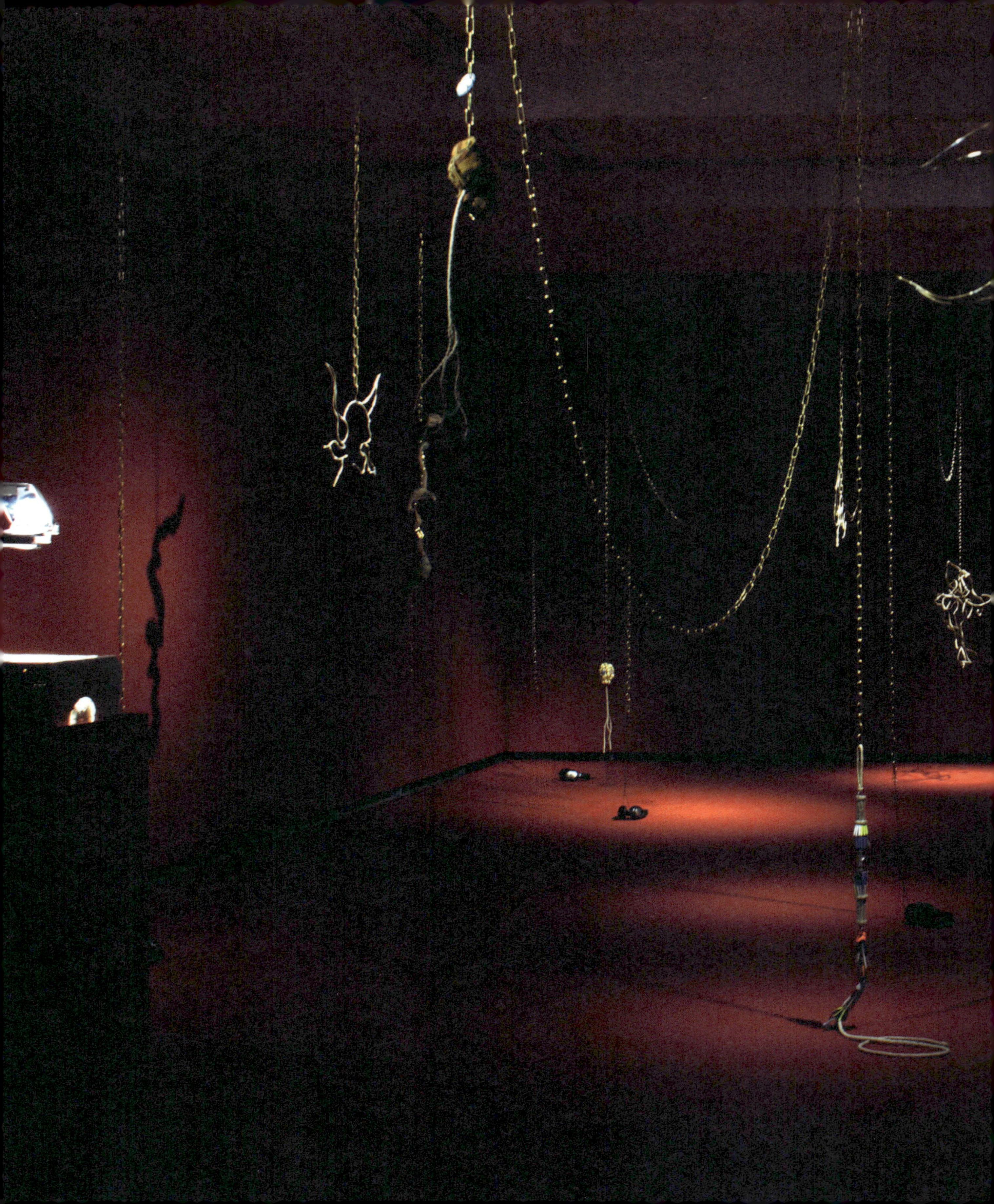

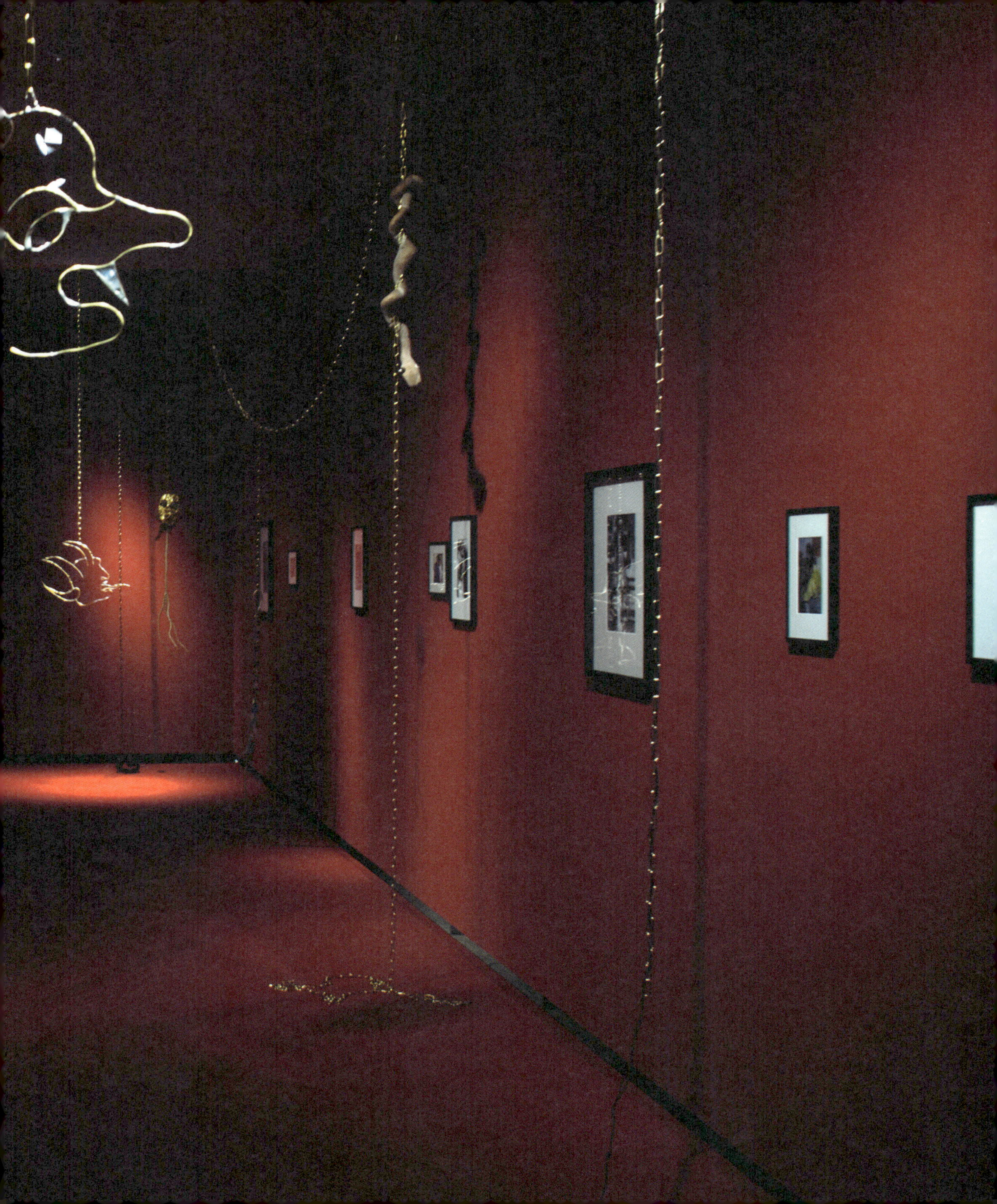

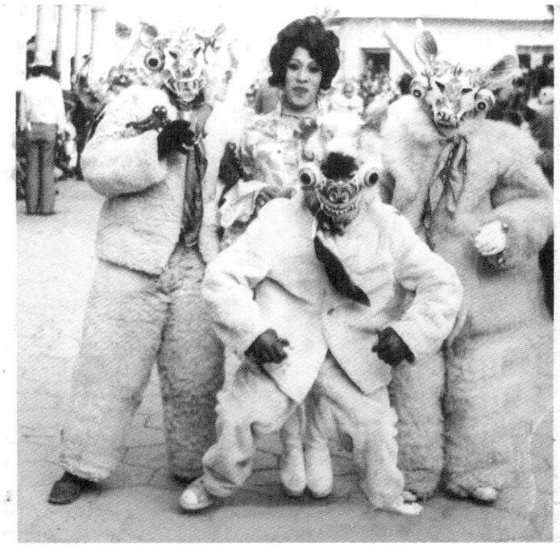

The following is a selection of images from the David Aruquipa Pérez-Comunidad Diversidad Archive regarding the performances of *Chinas Morenas* during different festivities in the Bolivian Andes. Therefore, this first presentation of *Radio Carabuco* at Künstlerhaus Bethanien as well as these pages hope to serve as a small tribute to all of them: Ofelia, Danna Galán, Barbarella (†), Titina (†) and Liz Karina.

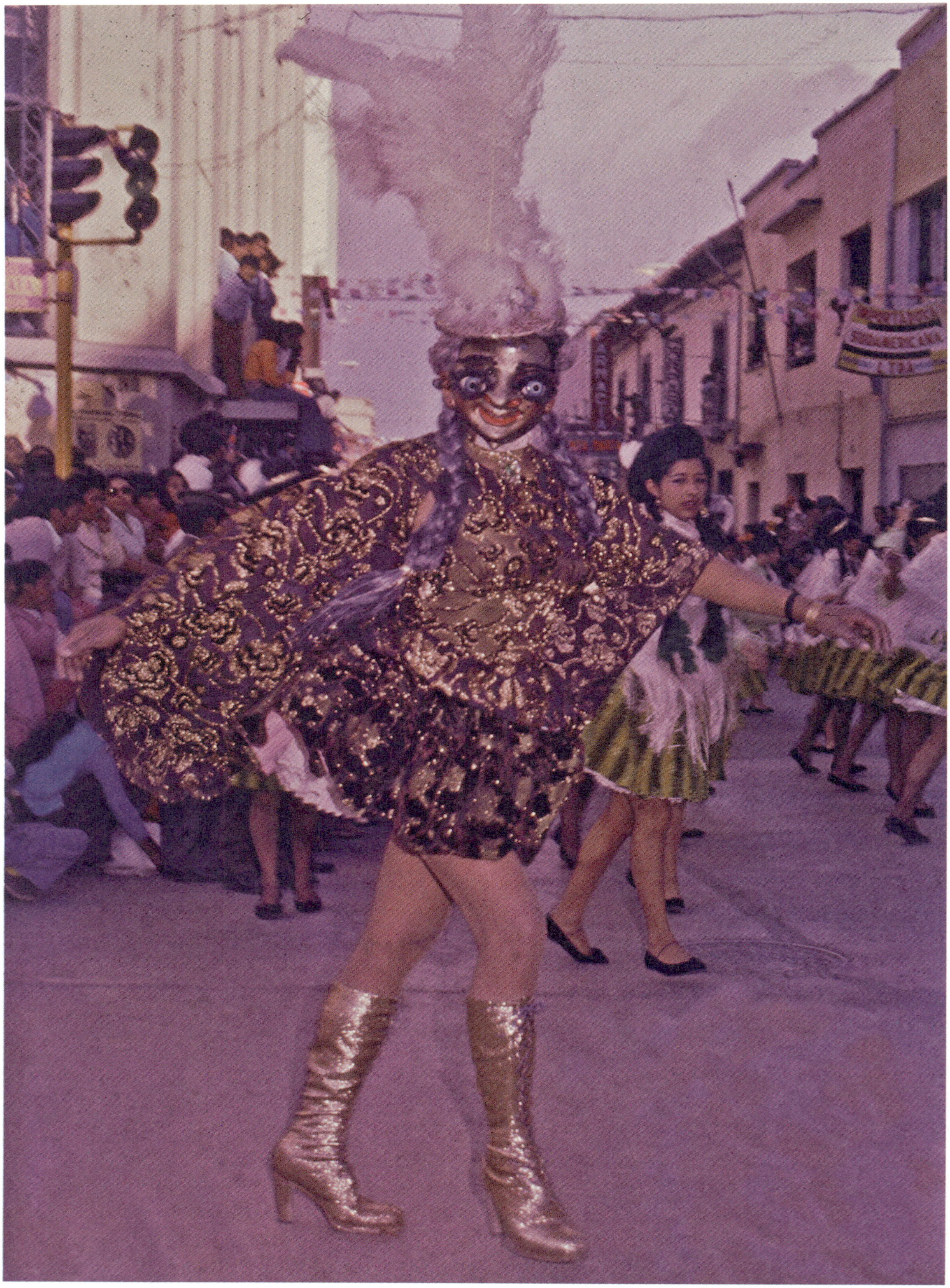

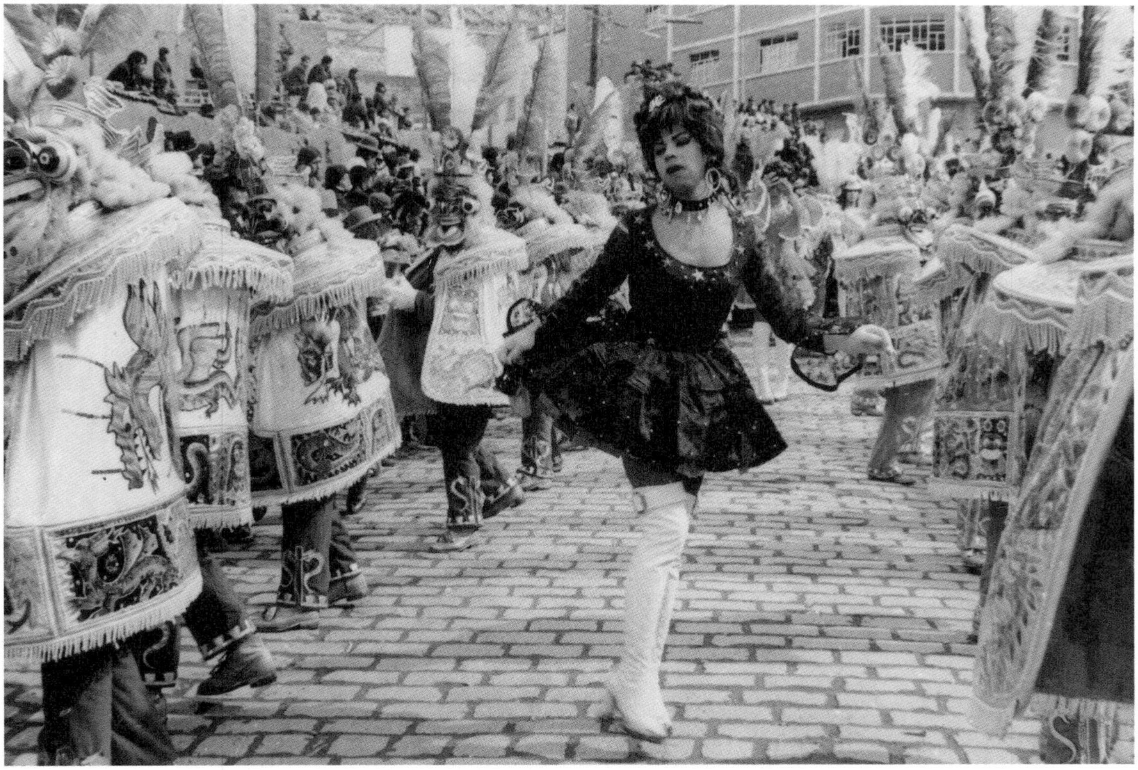

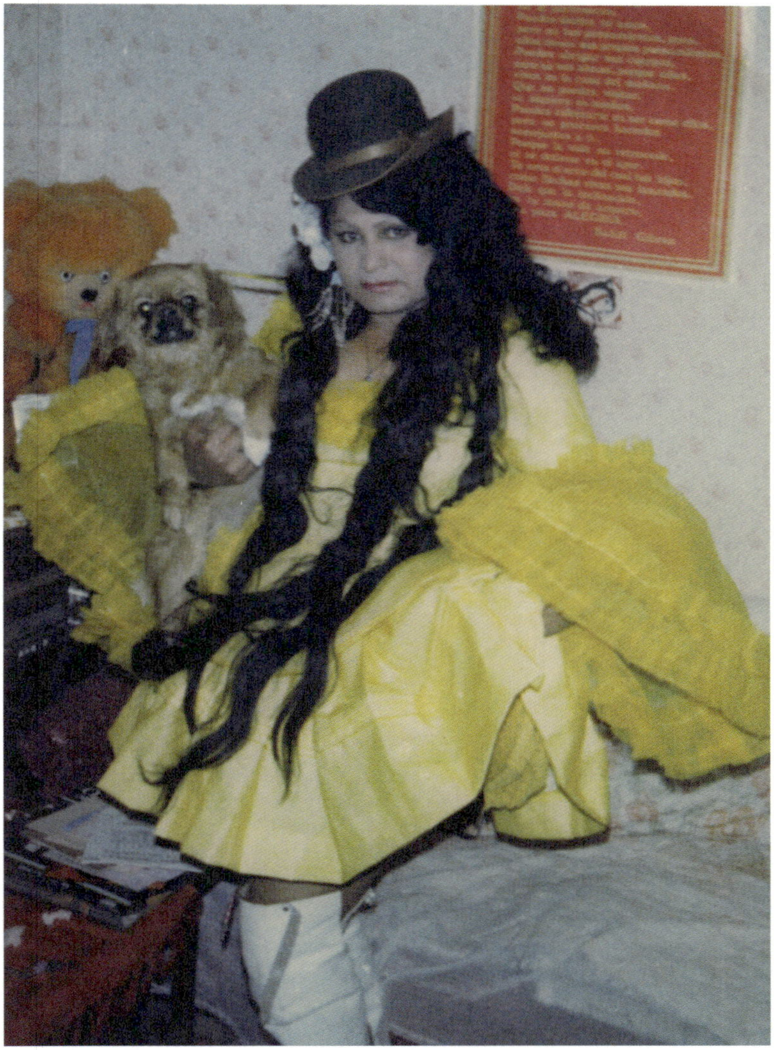

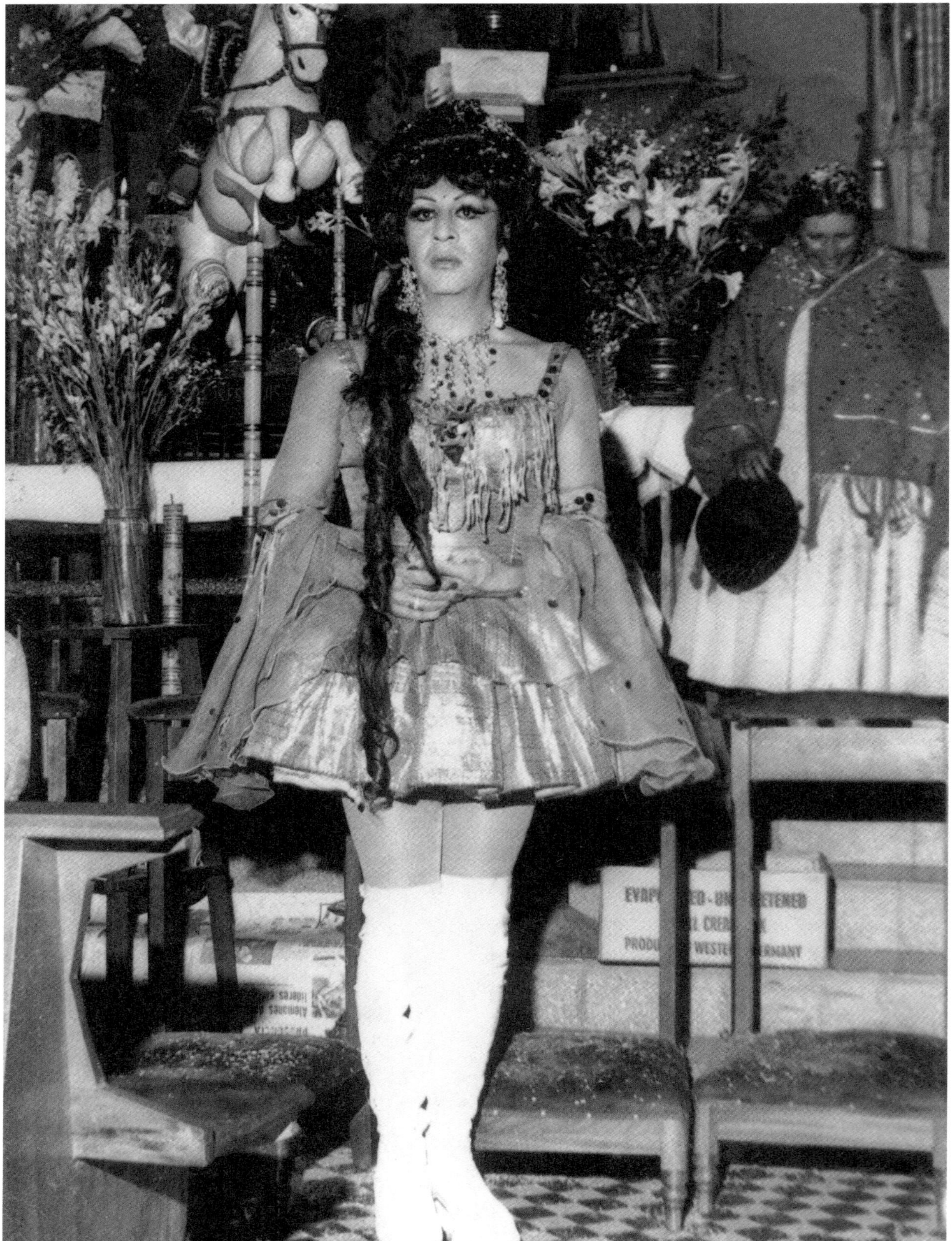

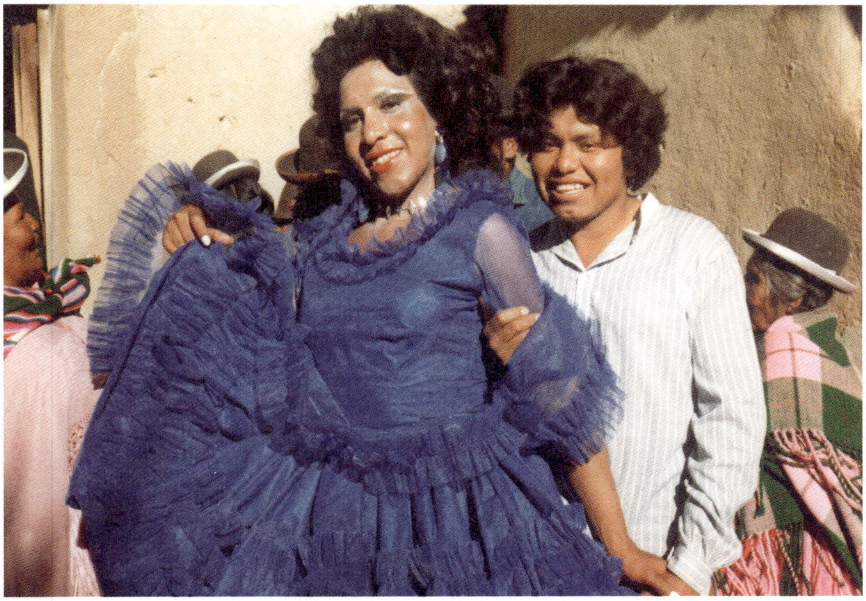

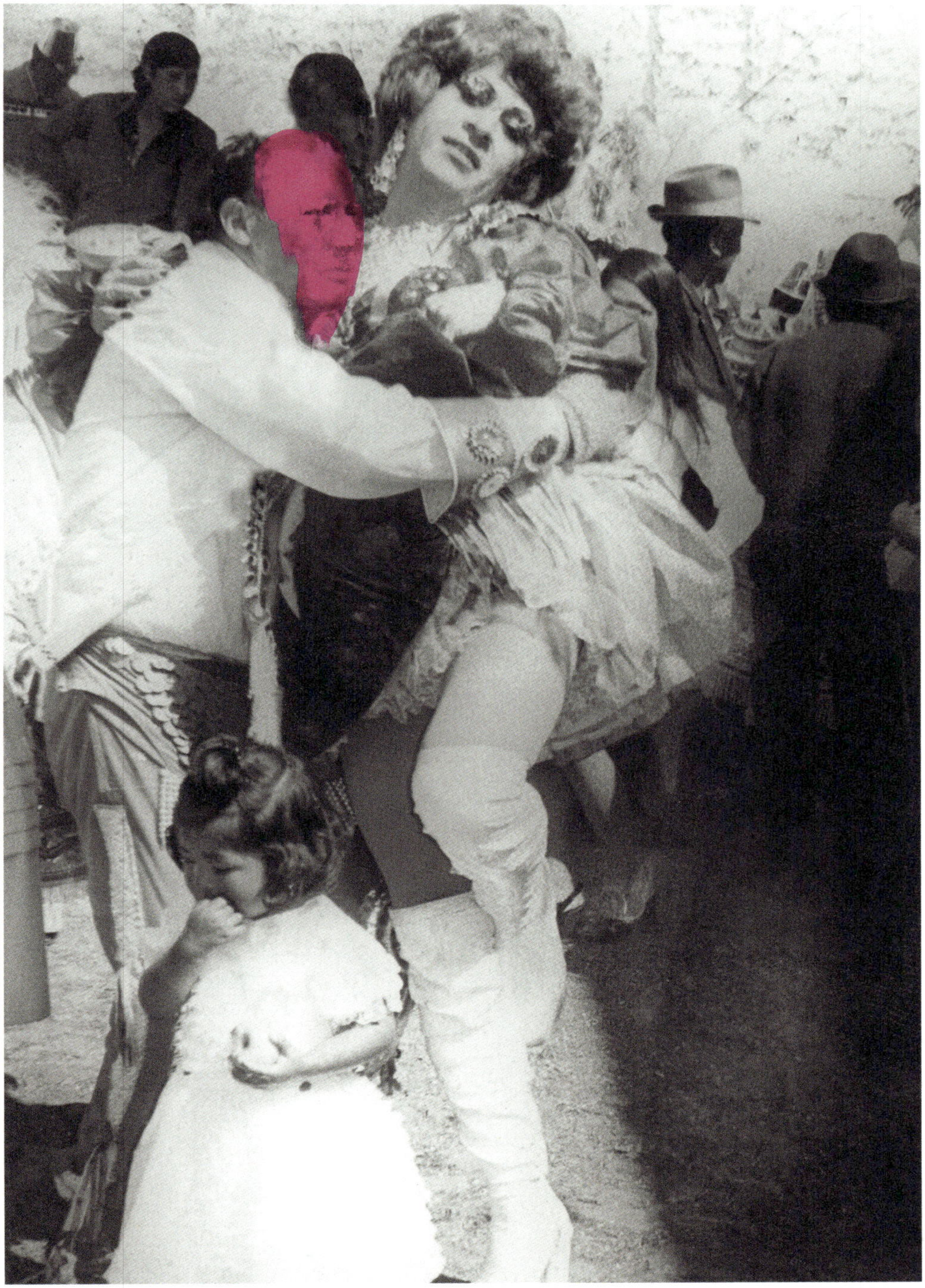

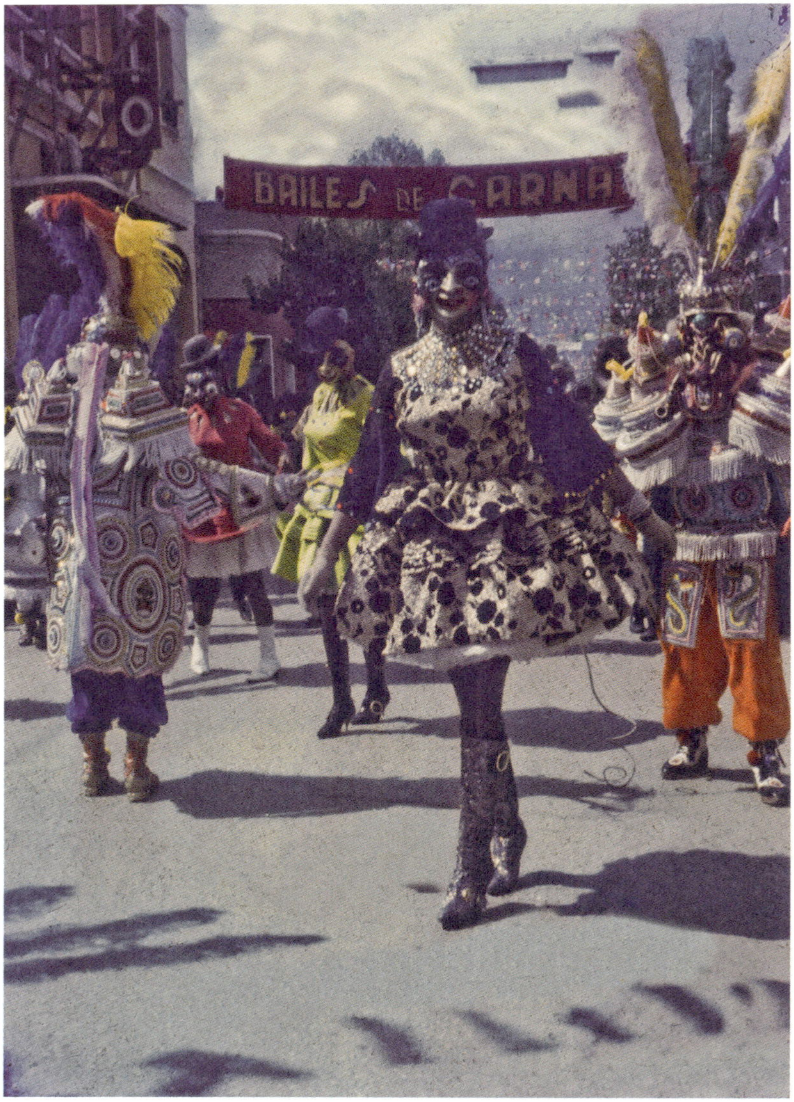
BAILES DE CARNA

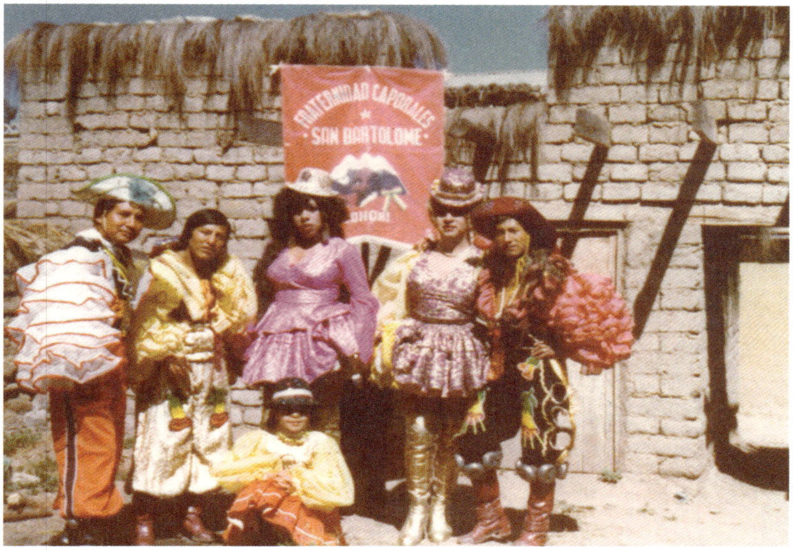
FRATERNIDAD CAPORALES
SAN BARTOLOME

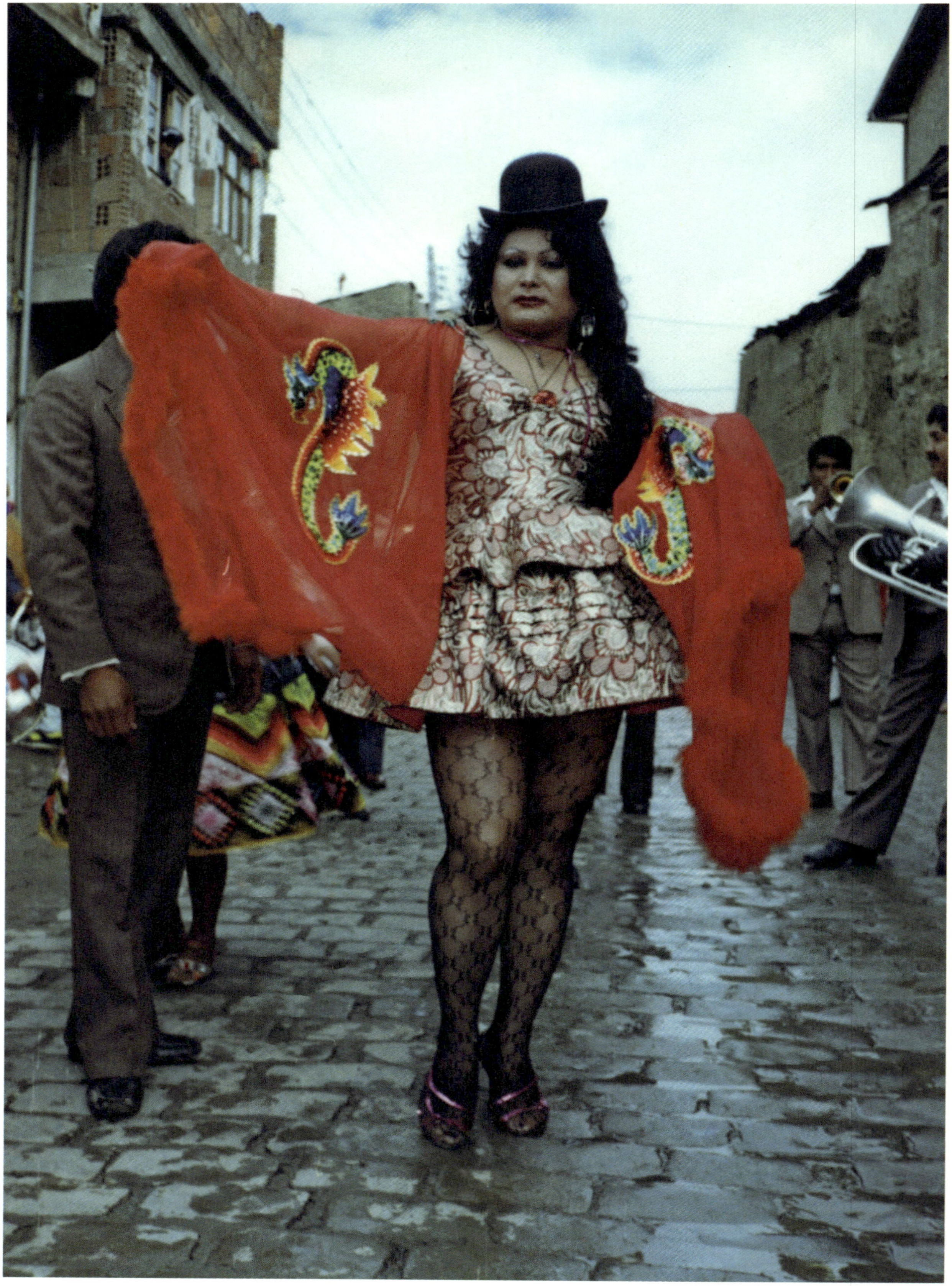

Bolivia: Historical Background

by Alfredo Coloma

Ever since its foundation, Bolivia has been on a quest to define a national identity. This quest could be understood as an effort to overcome the deeply fragmented nature of its society, which resulted mainly from the inheritance of a "feudal system" that had kept the indigenous majority in subordination since independence from Spain, but also from the deficient communication between the diverse regions of the country. As with most Latin American countries, the elites that controlled the early republican state aspired to build a nation according to the European archetype based on a homogenous population. This logically led to the exclusion of the indigenous population from actively participating in the process of construction of the new nation. In fact, they were considered to be an obstacle for its development and deemed as the "Indian problem".

During its first century of existence, Bolivia lost almost one half of its territory following different conflicts with its neighbouring countries. The War of the Pacific, which lasted from 1879 to 1884, resulted in the loss of sovereign access to the Pacific Ocean. This crippling defeat not only had devastating effects on the economy of the country but also on its population's morale. The trauma left by the war in the collective psyche still lingers until this day. The period after the war was marked by internal political struggles between the ruling elites, which led to a civil war in 1899. Known as the Federal War, it brought the Liberal Party to power and resulted in the transfer of the seat of power from Sucre to La Paz. An alliance formed between the Liberals and certain indigenous groups was crucial to the defeat of the Conservative Party. Under the leadership of the Aymara leader, Pablo Zárate "Willka", an indigenous army was raised among the peasants of La Paz and its mobilisation spread from La Paz to Oruro, Cochabamba and Potosí, representing the biggest indigenous military activity since colonial times.

Nevertheless, once the Liberals had achieved victory, "they not only abandoned federalism [...], but they also sent troops to disarm the Indians and imprisoned their leaders, thus violently suppressing the Indian mobilization."[1]

1 Herbert S. Klein, *A Concise History of Bolivia*, Cambridge University Press, 2003, New York, p. 157.

Following this revolt, the "Indian problem" became ever more present at the beginning of the 20th century and the governing elites sought desperately to resolve it. European scientific experts, brought to the country in an effort to study and understand the Indians, proclaimed them "fit to become the nation's productive peasants, mineworkers, and soldiers, but essentially unfit for participation in public culture and politics."[2] Many educational projects seeking a subordinate integration of the Indians, as peasants, soldiers or miners, were thus developed during the first two decades of the 20th century.

Indigenism, which spread in Latin America since the 1920s, marked a moment of redefinition of the indigenous population as it sought its integration in society. This aspiration came "from the need to widen the limits of the Nation by incorporating the 'other' who was previously excluded, [...] but without renouncing to the idea of an exclusive and ethnically homogeneous Nation. This way, ethnic pluralism is admitted (or rather denounced) as a fact, but not as a desirable condition for the future."[3]

The *Semana indianista* ("Indianist week"), held in 1931 in La Paz, was an event that sought to officially adopt Indigenism as the main current of thought in the Bolivian cultural field. It was organised by the *Amigos de la Ciudad* ("Friends of the City Association"), which was composed mainly of intellectuals and other public figures. The event, which took place between the 19th and the 27th of December, offered various activities such as conferences, concerts, debates etc. The expressed aim of the event was to rescue indigenous culture and spread it as the element that constituted the Bolivian singularity, not only within the city of La Paz, but above all to the international community. In this sense, "the meticulous representation of an autochthonous, rural Indian as a vestige of the past and a source of decorative motifs coexisted with the image of the "savage Indian" that persisted throughout the 19th century."[4] It is not surprising that it was during this event that Tiwanaku was presented as the birthplace of Bolivian identity.

Notorious archaeologist Bruce Trigger stated that nationalistic archaeology's main function is to "bolster the pride and morale of nations or ethnic groups. It is probably strongest amongst peoples who feel politically threatened [...], or in countries where appeals for national unity are being made to counteract serious divisions along class lines."[5] This definition seems to fit particularly well to the historical development of archaeology in Bolivia.

Even though the Tiwanaku ruins have been of interest ever since the country's foundation, it was in the 1930s that the site's systematic exploration began. American archaeologist Wendell C. Bennett's 1932 mission was the first thorough study of the site's monuments and led to the discovery of one of its most significant elements, a 24-feet-high monolith carved from a single block of red sandstone. Named after its discoverer, the monolith became of great interest to Arthur Posnansky, an Austrian naval engineer who had been Tiwanaku's most prolific scholar up to that point. He considered Tiwanaku to be the preeminent and most ancient metropolis of the ancient Americas.[6] Well respected by the local intellectual circle, he encouraged Bolivians to incorporate Tiwanaku motifs into their art and was the originator of the neo-Tiwanaku architectural style by designing the National Bolivian Museum in 1922.

2 Brooke Larson, *Trials of Nation Making: Liberalism, Race, and Ethnicity in the Andes, 1810–1910*, Cambridge University Press, 2004, Cambridge, p. 239.

3 Cecilia Warren, "La creación de la *Semana indianista*. Indianidad, Folklore y Nación en Bolivia", in *Universitas Humanística*, January–June 2014, Bogota, p. 174.

4 Ibid., p. 188.

5 Bruce Trigger, "Alternative archaeologies: Nationalist, colonialist, Imperialist", in *MAN*, New Series Vol. 19, No. 3, Sep. 1984, p. 360.

6 Arthur Posnansky, *Tiahuanaco: The Cradle of American Man*, J. J. Augustin, 1945, New York.

Convinced that the recently discovered monolith needed to be preserved and appreciated by future generations in the urban centres, Posnansky carried out negotiations to transport the monolith to the city of La Paz. After the approval of the authorities, the Bennett monolith was moved from its original location and placed on the city's most prominent avenue, El Prado. Nevertheless, the arrival of the monolith caused a commotion and was the subject of heated protests. "The newspapers of the time were filled with accounts of people voicing their outrage against such an imposition, they called it a 'piece of rock' bound to bring trouble, and an ugly reminder of a useless pre-civilized past."[7]

In 1940, the Bennett monolith was relocated to the *Plaza del Hombre Americano* ("The American Man Plaza"), which was designed by Posnansky. The plaza was built on a terrain adjoining La Paz's football stadium, which also featured Tiwanaku iconography on its façade. Located in the neighbourhood of Miraflores, the plaza was a replica of the semi-subterranean temple of Tiwanaku, in which the Bennett monolith was set as the centrepiece. However, the neighbourhood residents publicly opposed the monolith's transfer, arguing that the Andean spirits were not pleased with its uprooting and that it would bring them bad luck. Indeed, the monolith was never truly welcomed in La Paz, neither by the elites, who saw in it a reminder of their own Indianness, nor by the indigenous population, who saw its presence in the urban centre as a travesty.

After Posnansky's death in 1946, the growing nationalist movement eagerly embraced his view of Tiwanaku as a glorious past uniting all Bolivians. The nationalists sought to integrate the subordinated indigenous population by turning them into producers and assigning them the role of *campesinos* (peasants). Soon after the National Revolution of 1952 that brought the nationalists to power, important steps were taken by the Bolivian government to institutionalise archaeology, as part of its strategy to integrate the indigenous population into the country's social life. At the head of the state-funded *Centro de Investigaciones Arqueológicas Tiwanaku* (Centre for Tiwanaku Archaeological Research), archaeologist Carlos Ponce Sanjines directed the reconstruction of the archaeological site and published several essays and books. "A self-proclaimed pioneer and leader of this movement in which national identity was based on the disclosure and preservation of an Andean common past",[8] Ponce Sanjines stood at the head of this institution for more than four decades and is considered to be the most influential scholar in Bolivian archaeology. Thus, Tiwanaku was progressively adopted as the emblem of Bolivian identity during the second half of the 20th century.

It was only in 2002 that the Bennett monolith was moved back to Tiwanaku, coinciding with the emergence of an indigenous nationalism that would reconfigure Bolivia's sociopolitical structure. Indeed, with the arrival of Evo Morales to the presidency in 2006, Tiwanaku has once again been the focus of attention and a vehicle for nationalist ideology. This new nationalist period was in fact inaugurated by Morales's symbolical investiture as president in an Andean ritual at the archaeological site.

7 Isabel Scarborough, "The Bennett Monolith, Archaeological Patrimony and Cultural Restitution in Bolivia", in *The Handbook of South American Archaeology*, Springer, New York, pp. 1095–1101.

8 Ibid., p. 1097.

Andrés Pereira Paz: Three Works

by Alfredo Coloma

The following is a selection of works done by myself with artist and writer Alfredo Coloma based on what we thought would be the current nervous system of my body of work. After really in-depth conversations, we have chosen works that may give more leads to some subjects in my current practice. I hope you enjoy all the references I've been addressing as much as I do.
I would also like to invite everyone who does art to enjoy their own art history as I do. The Western world needs to stop imposing a common/canonical art history. Diversity involves contradiction, and contradiction, as once a great artist said, is freedom.

Andrés Pereira Paz

Felipe Guamán Poma de Ayala's chronicle *La Primer Nueva Corónica y Buen Gobierno* ("The First New Chronicle and Good Government") is the historical source for Pereira Paz's series *Guamán*. This chronicle was produced between 1612 and 1615 and written in the form of a 1198-page letter comprising more than 300 black ink drawings. As its title suggests, it is divided in two parts. "The first, entitled *Nueva Corónica*, is devoted to the history of the indigenous world before the *conquista*; The second part, entitled *Buen Gobierno*, depicts the society of the Viceroyalty of Peru under the reign of Viceroy Toledo: it makes a mockery of the concept of *good government*."[1] Guamán Poma addressed the chronicle to King Felipe III of Spain, in the hope of improving colonial rule, but it is unlikely that it ever got into the king's hands.

In her 2010 text "Sociología de la imagen: Una visión desde la historia colonial andina" ("Sociology of the Image: A View from Andean Colonial History"), Bolivian sociologist Silvia Rivera affirms that "images offer us social interpretations and narratives [...] and offer us perspectives for a critical understanding of reality."[2] From her perspective, images allow us to discover "senses not censored by the official language".[3] Considering Guamán Poma's chronicle, she affirms that, more than in his texts, "it is in the drawings that the chronicler displays his own ideas about the pre-Hispanic indigenous society [...] and the meanings of the hecatomb represented by the colonization."[4]

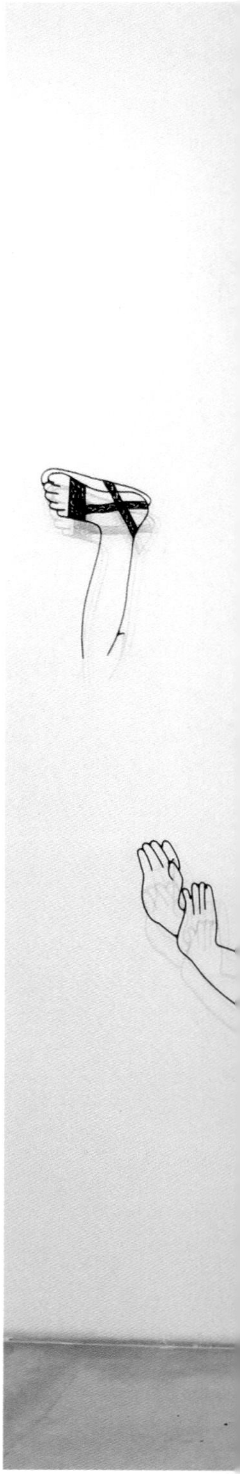

1 Alice Creischer, Max Jorge Hinderer, Andreas Siekmann (eds.), *The Potosí Principle. How Can We Sing the Song of the Lord in an Alien Land?*, Verlag der Buchhandlung Walther König, 2010, Cologne, p. 95.

2 Silvia Rivera, "Sociología de la imagen. Una visión desde la historia colonial andina", in *Ch'ixinakax utxiwa. Una reflexión sobre prácticas y discursos descolonizadores*, Tinta Limón, 2010, Buenos Aires, p. 20.

3 Ibid., p. 21.

4 Ibid., p. 22.

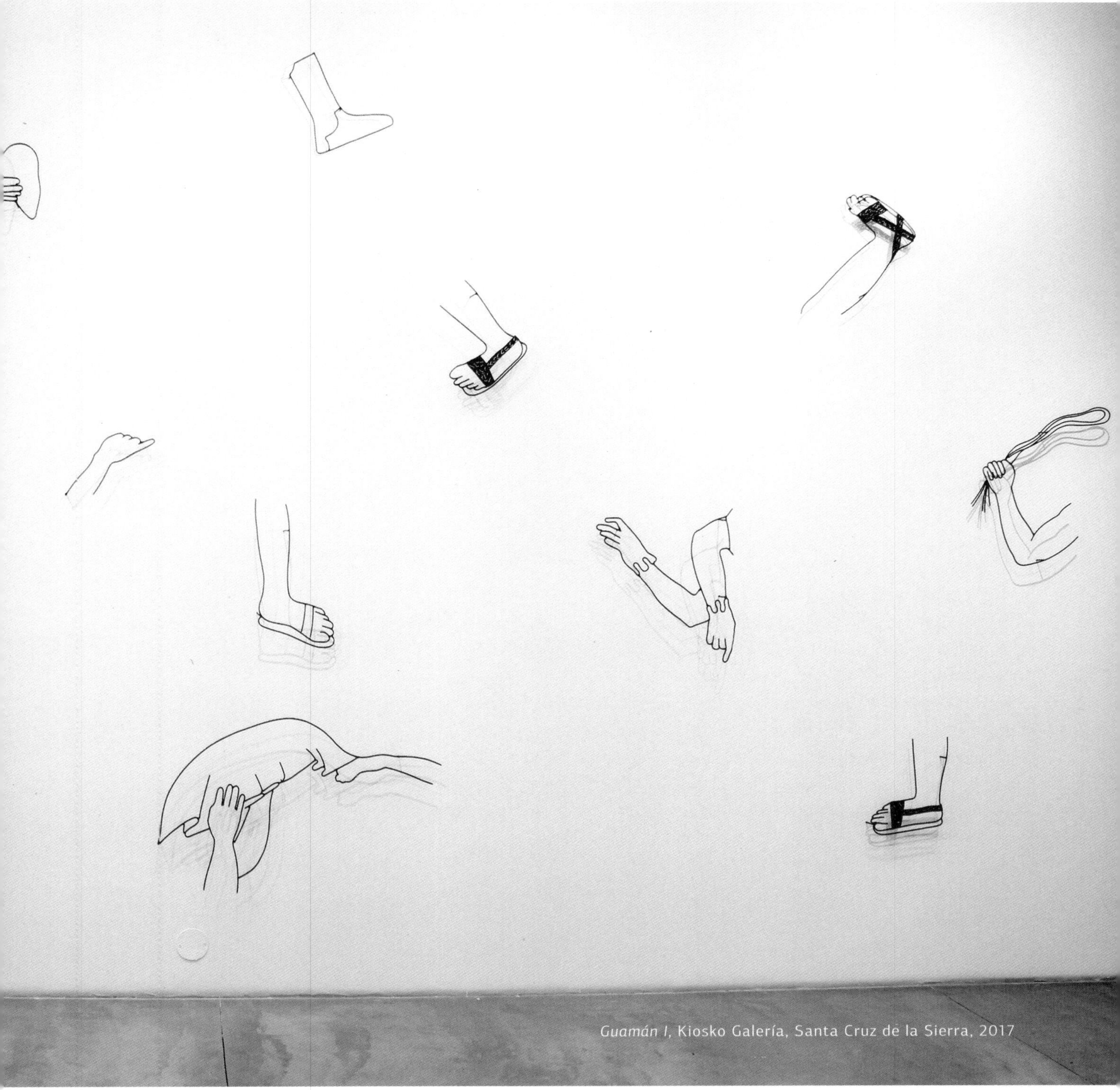

Guamán I, Kiosko Galería, Santa Cruz de la Sierra, 2017

From a position analogous to Rivera's concerning Guamán Poma's drawings, Pereira Paz focuses on some of their graphic elements and tries to highlight their symbolic potential. To this end, he has extracted and magnified them by transforming them into galvanized-wire wall reliefs. In *Guamán I* (2016–2017), Pereira Paz focuses on certain body extremities of some of the characters depicted in Guamán Poma's drawings. Decontextualised and rearranged in a more or less disorganised configuration, the gestures represented by these extremities become evident and echo the prevailing violence and chaos of the colonial period. In *Guamán II* (2017), Pereira Paz's attention shifts to the recurring presence of religious symbols in Guamán Poma's drawings, both pre-Columbian and Catholic. By gathering and displaying them on the same background, the confrontation between these different cosmogonies as well as the state of confusion that resulted from it become apparent.

For *Guamán III* (2018), Pereira Paz was inspired by two specific drawings depicting the executions of Atahualpa (1533), the last Inca Emperor, and Tupac Amaru (1572), the last indigenous monarch of the Neo-Inca state. Though both Incas were executed in different ways, they are represented in an almost identical manner in the drawings. Both Atahualpa and Tupac Amaru "lie down, their bodies oriented in the same direction, while a Spaniard cuts off their heads with a large knife and another one holds them by the feet."[5] Guamán Poma was indeed not interested in an accurate representation of these events, but more in what they came to represent for the fate of his people. Pereira Paz's selection of gestures, by their circular disposition, amplifies the symbolism of the original drawings and thus points out the systematic killing of the indigenous population undertaken by the colonisers.

In the latest work of the series, *Guamán IV: Astrónomo y poeta* (2018), Pereira Paz extracts two main features, a hat and a cane, out of the peculiar indigenous astrologer-poet represented in one of Guamán Poma's drawings. By focusing on these two symbols, Pereira Paz highlights the high esteem the chronicler had for this character, who was envisioned as a bearer of the knowledge of indigenous people and thus as an agent of resistance to the colonial cultural imposition. In the words of Silvia Rivera, "this is a poet, in the Aristotelian sense of the term: creator of the world, producer of food, master of the cycles of the cosmos."[6]

5 Ibid., p. 31.

6 Ibid., p. 33.

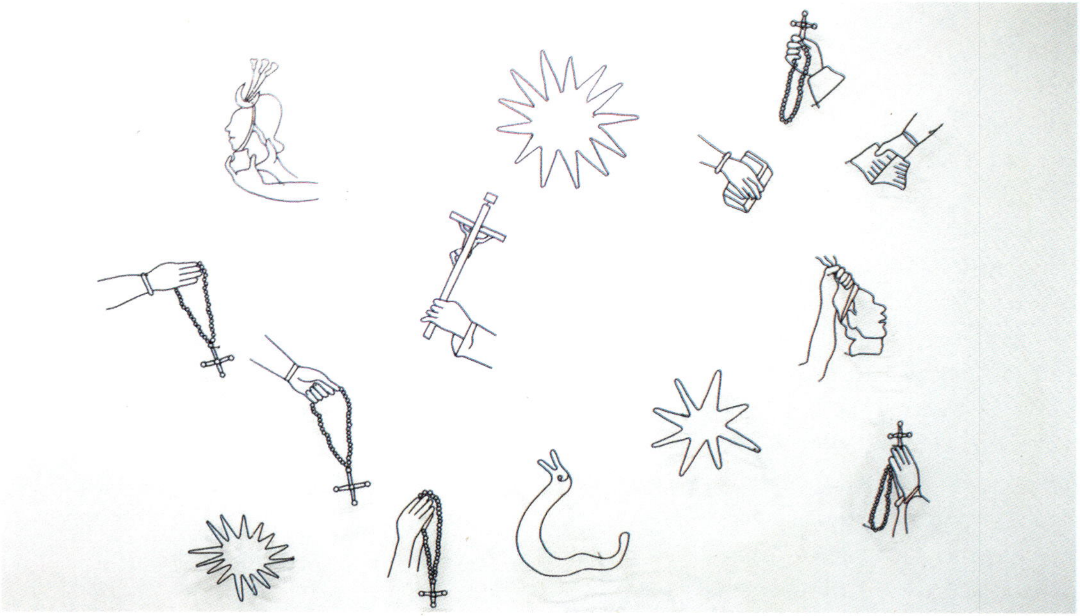

Guamán II, Dot Fiftyone Gallery, Miami, 2018

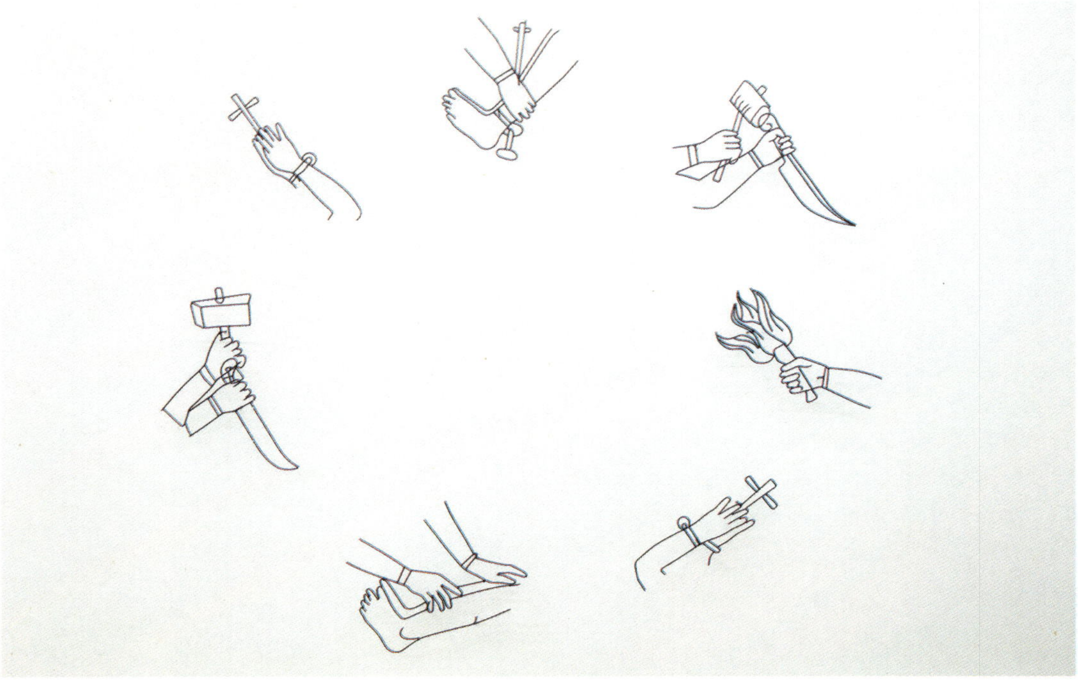

Guamán III, The Ryder Gallery, London, 2018

While living in Lima, Pereira Paz expanded his interest in indigenous iconography by focusing on the local cultural history. For his 2017 work *Conductas y adhesiones: Izcue*, Pereira Paz takes a historical element from Peruvian art history as its basis: Peruvian artist Elena Izcue's 1926 book "El Arte peruano en la escuela" ("Peruvian Art in School"). Izcue's book features more than thirty pre-Columbian designs as graphic models. Its aim was to introduce them as foundational elements in schoolchildren's artistic education while promoting the country's national identity at the same time. Produced in Lima between 1924 and 1925, the book was actually published in Paris and in three different languages. Although this might seem paradoxical, especially considering Izcue's alignment with Indigenism, it illustrates quite well the general fondness artists and intellectuals had for the artistic capital at the time, as well as their ambition to integrate it.

Pereira Paz uses Izcue's book as it was originally intended, that is, as a guide from which graphic elements can be extracted and applied. Thus, he selected some of the pre-Columbian motifs from the book and embroidered them on a found vintage blanket, which happens to feature another pre-Columbian figure in the Andean region, the infamous *Inti* or the "Sun God". The resulting superposition of pre-Columbian motifs generates a sort of *mise-en-abîme* that puts their origin into question. Pereira Paz's intervention points to the vacuity of meaning produced by using these designs as autonomous decorative elements. Izcue's clustering of pre-Columbian designs leads in fact to the idea of a "general and coherent cultural matrix that abolishes the heterogeneity of the styles of pre-Columbian Peru and affirms, at the same time, the existence of a 'Peruvian art'."[7]

7 Natalia Majluf, Luis Eduardo Wuffarden, *Elena Izcue, Lima-Paris, Années 30*, Flammarion, 2008, Paris, p. 22.

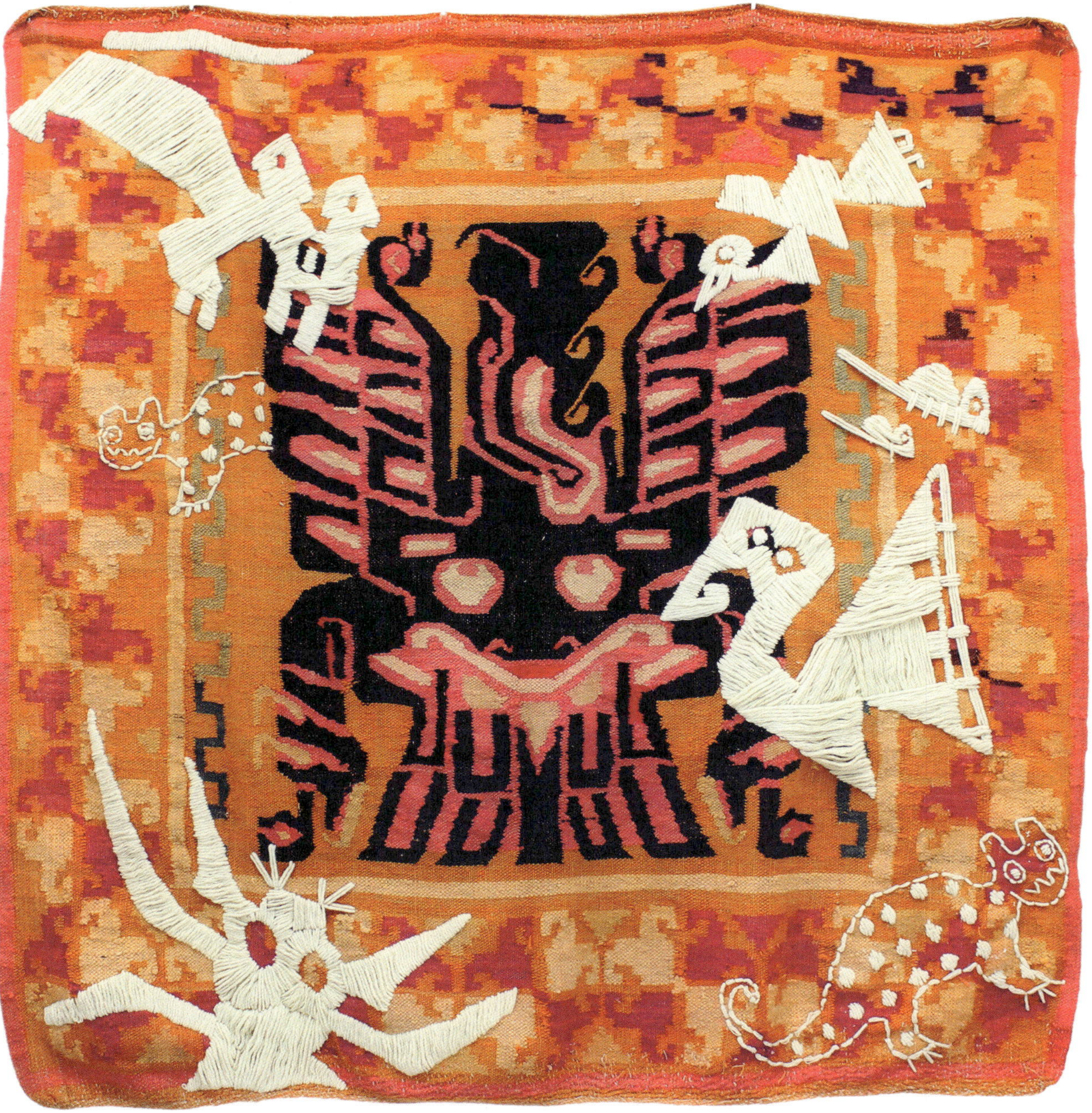

Manners and accessions: Izcue, 2017

For his 2018 sculpture, *Metafísica en Los Andes: Un yatiri va a la costa* ("Metaphysics in the Andes: A Yatiri goes to the Coast"), Pereira Paz took inspiration from *Yatiri* (1918), an emblematic painting by Arturo Borda (1883–1953), who was one of Bolivia's most relevant artists of the 20th century. Borda's painting depicts a Yatiri, an Aymara traditional healer, reading the fortunes of three indigenous women in coca leaves. "Borda's work in this genre represented the first initiative in (Bolivian) art to deal with such subjects and marked the beginning of a gradual recognition by members of the elite of the values inherent in the alienated native cultures."[8] Nevertheless, Borda became critical of Indigenism in his later years and came to consider it as a "vapid and lifeless movement which actually betrayed the Indians and undermined their cultural, social and economic revitalization".[9] By this, Borda referred to the way indigenous people had been considered only as representatives of a distant past and not as active participants in the development of society.

With his sculpture, Pereira Paz prolongs the history of representations of the Yatiri initiated by Borda. However, he departs from this legacy by means of a prospective take on this character. By emulating an ethnographic museum display, the extremities that compose the sculpture propose a projective consideration of the Yatiri. The baroque inclusion of marine elements on them induces a reading in which the traditional healer would have abandoned the Andean territory and reached the ocean. Pereira Paz proposes thus a reconsideration of this emblematic character by placing him in a hypothetic futuristic scenario instead of in a definite one in the past.

8 Pedro Querejazu, "Bolivia", in Edward Sullivan (ed.), *Latin American Art in the Twentieth Century*, Phaidon Press, 1996, London, p. 237.

9 Ibid., p. 238.

Yatiri va a la costa, 2018

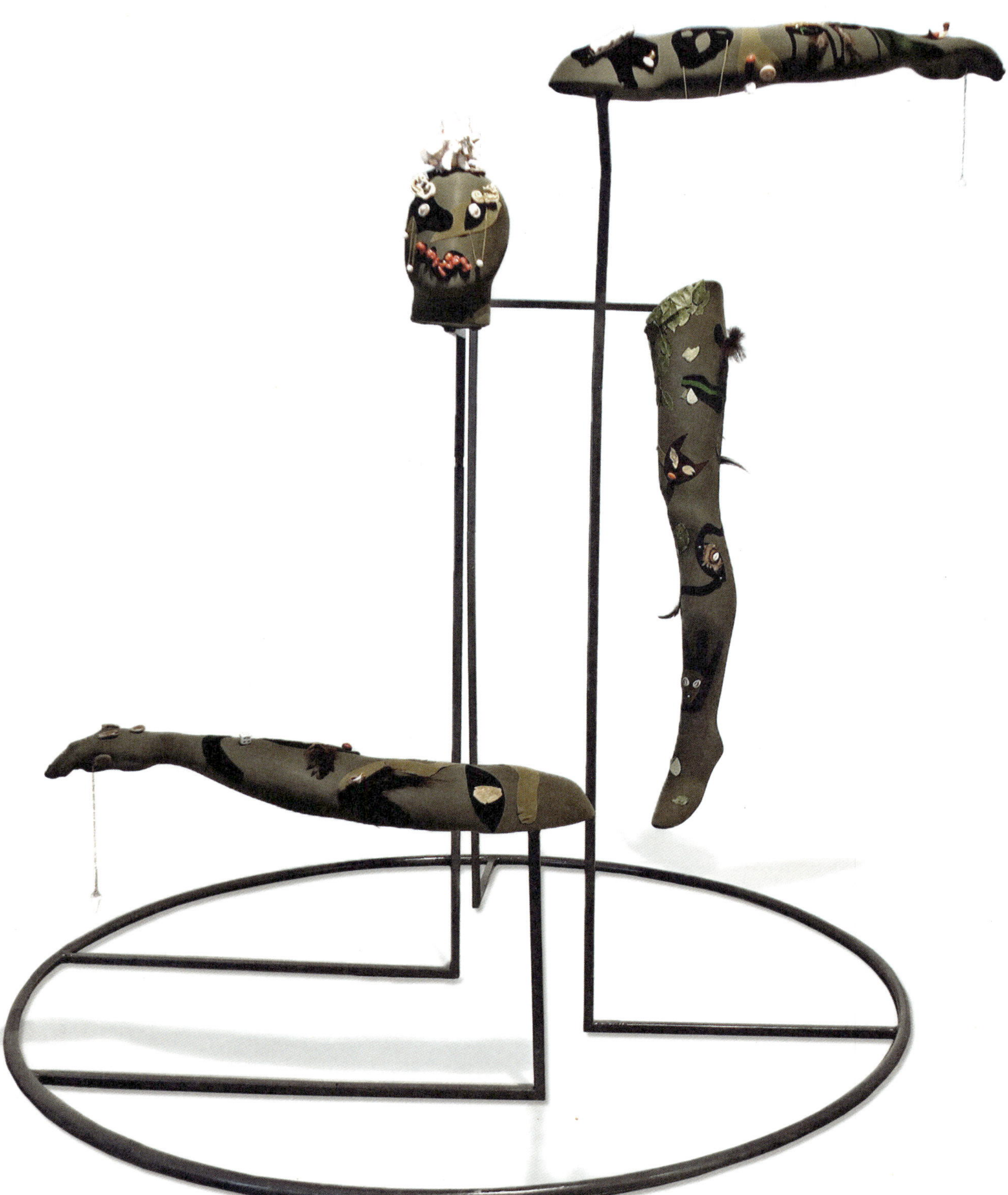

List of Works

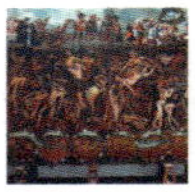 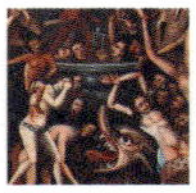 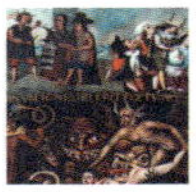

José López de los Ríos, ***El Infierno***, ca. 1664
Oil on canvas, 6.64 x 3.35 m
© Carlos Rúa Landa, Taller National de Restauración de Bolivia, Ministrerio de Cultura e Turismo

Radio Carabuco, 2019
Logo by Andrés Pereira Paz

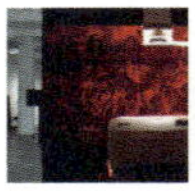 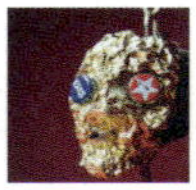 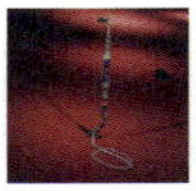 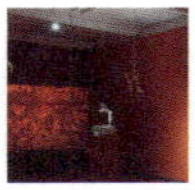 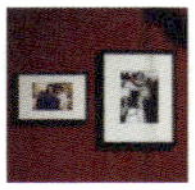 

Andrés Pereira Paz, ***Radio Carabuco,*** installation views, 2019
Brass sculptures, fabric sculptures, chains, whips, llama leather, audio installation, various dimensions
© Andrés Pereira Paz

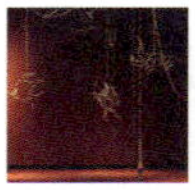 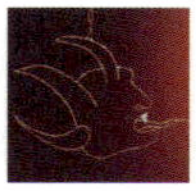 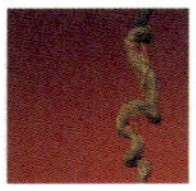

Andrés Pereira Paz, ***Radio Carabuco,*** installation views, 2019
© Künstlerhaus Bethanien, David Brandt

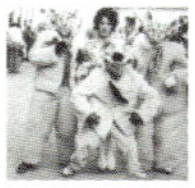 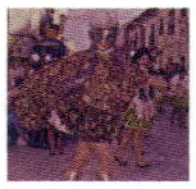 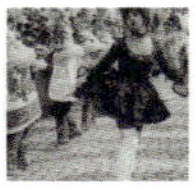 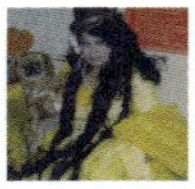 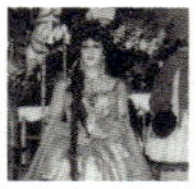 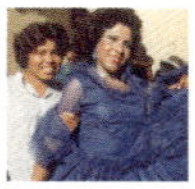 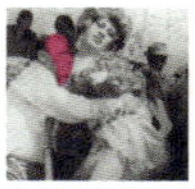 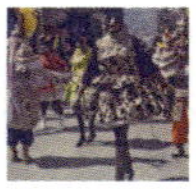 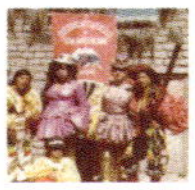 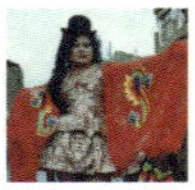

Selection of archive images for ***Radio Carabuco,*** 2019
© Archivo Comunidad – Diversidad David Aruquipa Pérez

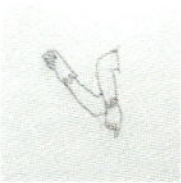 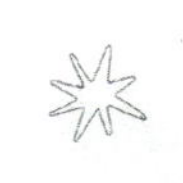 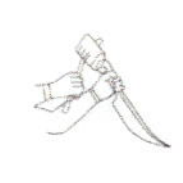

Andrés Pereira Paz, ***Guamán I,*** 2017, ***Guamán II & III,*** 2018
Galvanized wire, multiple dimensions
© Andrés Pereira Paz

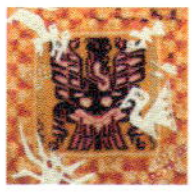

Andrés Pereira Paz, ***Manners and accessions: Izcue,*** 2017
Hand embroidered vintage recuay weave, 1.65 x 1.76 m
© Andrés Pereira Paz

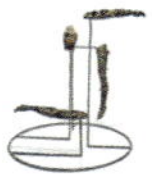

Andrés Pereira Paz, ***Yatiri va a la costa,*** 2018
Steel, different fabrics, seeds and hand embroidery, 1.50 m diameter x 1.70 m height
© Andrés Pereira Paz

About the authors:

Revd Dr Richard Davey is a Senior Visiting Research Fellow in the School of Art and Design at Nottingham Trent University, UK, where he is also the coordinating Chaplain. His research focuses on the work of contemporary art and artists as a lens through which to experience the nature of Being in the world, particularly concentrating on aspects of colour, line, space and spirituality. He has written numerous books and exhibition catalogues on international artists including Anselm Kiefer, Tess Jaray and Ed Moses for publishers and galleries such as the Royal Academy of Arts, London, and the Walker Gallery, Liverpool.

Alfredo Coloma is a Bolivian artist. He holds a BFA in Visual Art from Université Paris VIII (Paris, France) and a MFA (Hons.) in Visual Media from École Nationale Supérieure de la Photographie (Arles, France). He is currently pursuing a Master in Fine Art at HEAD – Genève, Haute Ecole d'Art et de Design (Geneva, Switzerland). In 2017 he was awarded the *Yvon Lambert Prize for Young Creation* by the Lambert Collection (France). He works between Geneva and La Paz.

Biography

Andrés Pereira Paz
Born in La Paz in 1986
Lives and works in Berlin

EDUCATION

2013 Center for Artistic Research, Buenos Aires, Argentina
2013 Tres de Febrero National University, Buenos Aires, Argentina
2009 Hernando Siles National Art Academy, La Paz, Bolivia

Among others, assistant to the workshops of Roberto Valcárcel and Diana Aisenberg

RESIDENCIES

2018–19 Künstlerhaus Bethanien, Berlin, Germany
2018 Kiosko, Santa Cruz de la Sierra, Bolivia
2017 HAWAPI, Tacna, Peru
2017 Gasworks, London, United Kingdom
2013 Centro Hipermediático Experimental Latinoamericano CheLA, Buenos Aires, Argentina

SELECTED SOLO EXHIBITIONS

2019 *Journey of the Anonymous*, House of Egorn Gallery, Berlin, Germany
2019 *Radio Carabuco*, Künstlerhaus Bethanien, Berlin, Germany
2018 *Salón Santa Cruz*, Kiosko Galería, Santa Cruz de la Sierra, Bolivia
2018 *Blue eyes*, curated by Aina Pomar, The Ryder Projects, London, United Kingdom
2018 *Rayo Purita or the future is what we carry on our back*, Crisis Galería, Lima, Peru
2017 *Open Studios*, Gasworks, London, United Kingdom
2016 *Roomate*, curated by Rodrigo Quijano, Kiosko Galería, Santa Cruz de la Sierra, Bolivia
2016 *Pachapapi*, curated by Guillermo E. Rodriguez, La Estación Espacial, San Juan, Puerto Rico
2015 *Hotel Cosmos* (in collaboration with Juan Diego Tobalina), Sala Luis Miró Quesada Garland, Lima, Peru
2014 *Suicide at the Pão de Açucar - A Tribute to Emeterio Villamil de Rada*, Cultural Center of Brasil in Bolivia, La Paz, Bolivia
2013 *General Intellect*, Centro Hipermediático Experimental Latinoamericano CheLA, Buenos Aires, Argentina
2012 *Enthusiasm*, Nuevo Museo Energía de Arte contemporáneo LA ENE, Buenos Aires, Argentina

SELECTED GROUP EXHIBITIONS

2019 *Elia Nurvista & Andrés Pereira Paz*, hosted by KfW Stiftung, Villa 102, Frankfurt, Germany

2019 *Survival Kit*, Latvian Centre of Contemporary Art, Riga, Latvia

2018 *Fashion Week*, Kinderhook & Caracas, Berlin, Germany

2018 *HAWAPI the terrestrial triangle*, Centro Cultural Cerrillos, Santiago de Chile, Chile

2018 *Contextos* Biennale, National Museum of Art, La Paz, Bolivia

2016 *Second Grand Tropical Biennale*, curated by Marina Reyes Franco, Pablo León de la Barra, Stephan Benchoam and Juni Figueroa, San Juan, Puerto Rico

2016 *A kingdom of hours*, curated by Robert Leckie and Miguel A. López, Teorética, San José, Costa Rica

2014 *Chojcho men*, curated by José Ballivián, French Alliance Gallery, La Paz, Bolivia

2014 *Bolivia does not exist*, Cuatroh Gallery, New York, United States

2013 *To talk with the death ones*, Local Gallery, Santiago de Chile, Chile

2013 *Foundations* Performance Festival, Simón I. Patiño Foundation, Cochabamba, Bolivia

2013 *I am the other*, Plurinational Cultural Center of Santa Cruz de la Sierra, Santa Cruz de la Sierra, Bolivia

2012 *Organ*, 713 Contemporary Art Gallery, Buenos Aires, Argentina

2012 *Performatic Museum*, Nuevo Museo Energía de Arte contemporáneo LA ENE, Buenos Aires, Argentina

2012 *The Dispersion*, Centro de Investigaciones Artísticas, Buenos Aires, Argentina

2011 *Life as a cathodic emission*, Rayo Láser Gallery, Buenos Aires, Argentina

2011 *Un museo Chévere*, Encuentro Internacional Cheverista de Medellín (MDE'11), curated by Julieta Gonzáles, Museo La Ene and Pablo León de la Barra, Medellín, Colombia

2009 *From strength comes union*, National Museum of Art of Bolivia, La Paz, Bolivia (ANBA), La Paz

OTHER PROJECTS

www.bisagra.org

Andrés Pereira Paz – Radio Carabuco
With texts by Richard Davey and Alfredo Coloma
Editors: Daniela Leykam, Christoph Tannert

Künstlerhaus Bethanien GmbH, Kohlfurter Straße 41/43, Showroom: Kottbusser Str. 10, D-10999 Berlin, www.bethanien.de
Artistic Director: Christoph Tannert / **Administrative Director:** Andrea Boche
International Studio Programme: Valeria Schulte-Fischedick / **Press & PR:** Christina Sickert
Administration: Ute Werner / **Technical Staff:** Toni Lebkücher, Peter Rosemann

KfW Stiftung, Palmengartenstraße 5–9, D-60325 Frankfurt am Main, www.kfw-stiftung.de
Executive Director: Dr. Aischa Astou Saw / **Programme Manager Arts and Culture:** Daniela Leykam

Editing: Daniela Leykam, Valeria Schulte-Fischedick, Seda Pesen
Copy-editing and Translation: Stefan Hollstein, Aymone Rassaerts
Cover photo: David Brandt / **Production:** Druckerei Kettler, Bönen
Project Management/Design: Thorsten Probst / angenehme-gestaltung.de

Published by Verlag Kettler, Dortmund, www.verlag-kettler.de

This catalogue is published on the occasion of the exhibition *Radio Carabuco* by Andrés Pereira Paz, International Studio Programme, Künstlerhaus Bethanien, Berlin, 1 September 2018 – 1 September 2019. Andrés Pereira Paz is a grant holder of KfW Stiftung.

The artist would like to acknowledge: Gabriel Acevedo Velarde, Ana Alenso, Hugo de Almeida Pinho, David Aruquipa Pérez, Andrea Brandão, Marcos Brias, Deborah Calderón, Alfredo Coloma, Stasiek Czaplitzki, Richard Davey, Hayden Fowler, Tanya Gangarova, Stelios Kallinikou, Daniela Leykam, Talya Lubinsky, Julio Lugón, Ministry of Cultures of Bolivia, Nicola Müllerschön, Elia Nurvista, Valeria Paz, Florencia Portocarrero, Lucía Querejazu, Marina Reyes Franco, Matheus Rocha Pitta, Carlos Rua, Liv Schulman, Anika Schwarzlose, Chaveli Sifre, Kyoco Taniyama, Juan Diego Tobalina, Adrián Villanueva, Amaru Villanueva Rance, and the Künstlerhaus Bethanien team.

Publications in the book series so far: PARADISE / Thabiso Sekgala / January 2014, THE MADMAN SEES WHAT HE SEES / Carla Zaccagnini / March 2014, STORE IN A COOL AND DRY PLACE / Prajakta Potnis / November 2014, LIFE ON MARS / Stary Mwaba / March 2015, THE LAND BENEATH MY FEET / Khvay Samnang / September 2015, IN SILENCE / Nguyen Thi Thanh Mai / March 2016, INTENDING PROBABILITY / Salwa Aleryani / March 2017, AOS VENCEDORES AS BATATAS / Matheus Rocha Pitta / June 2017, EXIT – ENTRANCE / Orawan Arunrak / August 2017, ALL THAT IS SEEN AND UNSEEN / Vartan Avakian / January 2019, FEEDING THE SCENE / Elia Nurvista / July 2019

ISBN 978-3-86206-784-8

KÜNSTLERHAUS BETHANIEN KFW STIFTUNG